What Does God Want?

Thoughts on Christian Life

Stan E. DeKoven

What Does God Want?

ISBN: 978-1-61529-015-4

Published by:

Vision Publishing

Ramona, CA 92065

www.visionpublishingservices.com

1-800-9-VISION

All scripture references are taken from the
NASB version of the Bible unless otherwise noted.
Printed in the United States of America

Table of Contents

What Does God Want?

A study on the practice of a God filled life

Introduction

I was asked to preach a series of messages at a church in Fontana California, Fontana Christian Center International. A question had been rattling around in my mind, influencing my prayer "what do I really want?" One night I began to really think about what I wanted, only to realize how very selfish and in many ways irrelevant that question was/is. I instead asked the question, "What does God Want?", a much more germane question, and one worth exploring. It did not take much to begin to see that my focus of prayer, only too common in our highly me oriented culture, was truly the wrong direction. To be effective as a believer, I needed to be clear on what God wanted, with the intention of lining my life up with his divine intention, while helping others to do the same. Well, this work is designed to answer the more important question, at least to my satisfaction, and hopefully to the satisfaction of the Lord for the benefit of others.

One of the distinctions of the New Testament/First Century church was the dramatic change in behavior seen in the converts to Christianity. Men and women who were impacted by the gospel of Jesus Christ were changed from the inside out. Having been regenerated by the Holy Spirit, they manifested God's grace, which was liberally applied to their lives, experiencing a profound transformation of character. Thieves became generous givers (Zacheus), murders became martyrs (Paul), the timid became strong (Timothy); lives previously bent towards self and personal gain were now thoroughly oriented towards loving God and serving (loving) others. Such was, and is, the power of the gospel.

As the church began to grow, hundreds then thousands came into the church, from all walks of life. Some changed instantaneously, but most changed gradually as the adherent was introduced to the principles of God's Word. For the Hebrew believer, making right choices was based on a very rigid but clearly defined code of rules, most of which were in line with the Word of God. The transition was most likely more difficult for the average Gentile.

Our present day church, though different in outward appearances remains similar to First Century Christianity. Men and women raised in families with strong teaching backed by consistent demonstration of right/wrong ethical behavior need little teaching on social graces, ethical behavior or a right biblical orientation. The law (ethics) is written on the heart (this is not to say that salvation is not needed). However, in light of our current world of open dysfunctional families raised in a pluralistic, humanistic, materialistic world, ethical teaching to the saved is again (perhaps always has been) necessary for the church to again be seen as the salt and light of the world.

Focus of This Book

This book is written for Christians desiring to understand the biblical principles for ethical behavior in the world we live. Principles are presented, while avoiding (for the most part) specific ethical dilemmas or assuming to answer every problematic quandary. Further, it is hoped that the reader will gain a perspective and passion to see a return to biblical perspectives of life and conduct that will affect our prayer and service. James M. Houston, as presented in an article from Christianity Today[1], usefully translates Jewish philosopher Emmanuel Levinas's notion of ethics into an evangelical-friendly idiom: Ethics is about living in the presence of another person. Therefore, what the Christian says to God is not "Here are all the things I think or feel about you," but "Here I am; relate to me."

By definition, Christian Ethics is "the study and practice of moral conduct, as set forth in the Bible." The foundation and

---

[1] Copyright © 2007 Christianity Today

absolute authority on which the Christian must base all standards for faith and practice is the word of God. The true believer must never live by natural instincts or unenlightened conscience. God has given clear instructions as to how we must live our life on this earth. With Him there are no gray areas. Everything is either right or wrong, black or white. Ethics in general relies upon natural instincts and reason as its foundation. In <u>Christian Ethics</u>, however, we must act by the Word of God as the foundation for our decisions. Though from God's view all decisions appear to be clear and forthright; black and white, for us mere mortals, gray is often the color of the day. The Word of God provides ample guidance for life decisions... following His principles help us achieve an ethical life before God and the world.

Chapter 1

The Importance of Christian Ethics

As previously stated, the definition of Christian Ethics is: the study and practice of moral conduct, as set forth in the Bible.

Again, with God, everything is right or wrong, black or white; there are no gray areas. Sin is sweet to the doer, but we cannot successfully live by our natural instincts or conscience. To live the Christian life well, it is essential to act in accordance to a clear understanding and judicial usage of the Word of God.

Ethics in general differs from Christian Ethics, in that the Bible is not commonly referred to in university courses on the subject, but instead natural instincts and reason are relied upon. Christian Ethics has two divisions: theoretical and practical.

1. Theoretical – which applies to fundamental principles of what is ethical (right or wrong). In this book we will emphasize principles, as they can be universally applied in any environment, and within any given culture.

2. Practical – putting into action the principles found in the word of God in our daily conduct.

Both are important; neither is complete without the other. The theory may be beautiful; but unless it is applied to our lives, it remains devoid of life.

Further, Christian Ethics differs from psychology. Psychology deals with the mind, will and emotions, with special emphasis on various motivations as to why people act as they do in given circumstances and situations. Psychology, as with most philosophical systems, prides itself in being "value free", or thoroughly situational in its ethics. Thus, to the question "Why?" the answer is often complex and depends on the circumstances. Christian Ethics attempts to grapple with the ideals of what is right or wrong in terms of deeds, thoughts and actions. That is, Christianity in general believes there are moral absolutes, 10 Commandments not 10 Suggestions, and other imperatives found in scripture that are important; no, essential to life in this world. Christian Ethics deals directly with what I ought to do, regardless of what I feel to do. As Dr. Ken Chant, dear friend and mentor has stated (in my paraphrase version), God is less interested in our happiness than our holiness, and preachers of the Word should be equally concerned with the later over the former.

Christian Ethics differs from religion. The chief world religions – Buddhism, Islam, Hinduism, and others) contain limited true ethical teaching. In most world religion's, religion itself is the service and adoration of God or a god, as expressed through various forms of worship. Human conduct is not viewed as morally right or wrong, it is judged according to its exhortation or offense to their gods. Ethical behavior is of primary importance in the world views related to Judeo-Christian foundations. Of course, we must remember that having the correct Christian Ethics cannot "save" a man, for salvation comes only through repentance, and believing in the sacrifice of Christ on the cross and His glorious resurrection (Rom. 10:9,10). Hebrews 9:22 says, "without the shedding of blood" a man cannot be saved. Salvation is essential, and Ethics is the good "works" which a Christian must diligently perform (Titus 1:16; 2:7-14; 3:1,5,8,14), based upon the marvelous grace and mercy of our loving and forgiving God.

Chapter 2

The Ideal Society and Worldviews

What is an "Ideal" Society? What philosophy embraces a correct worldview? What does it matter?

There are many ideologies, or various systems of human thought regarding an ideal society. The fact is, ideas have consequences, as they determine the actions a person is likely to take, things allowed or disallowed in his or her life. Of course, from a Christian Worldview, the first or premier worldview is God's view. God rules and the people carry out His government (at least in design). This was the primary focus of Jesus' ministry and teaching, that the rule of God (the Kingdom) had come, embodied in Christ, and that His reign would be an everlasting reign, one in which mankind would play a significant role (see Is. 9: 6-7). A second (but not specifically biblical) form of society is Democracy, with its many variations. Democracy is a system of man in which the people rule, not God. Another prevalent system of thought is Socialism, with its variations. This is also a system of man's design which desires the same outcome as Christianity; a utopian society.

Books like Sir Thomas More's "Utopia", which provides a pattern or plan for a utopian socialist society, coincides with much of the worldview of the ancient Greek philosophers. Of course, neither Communism, Democracy nor Socialism are Christian or Christ centered philosophies. They can not "see" God's Kingdom, so they attempt to create their own through political means. No governmental system of philosophy is completely compatible with Christianity, though some systems are more conducive to the spread of the Good news than others.

Socialism and Communism would change society by destroying moral intuition and the existing society and rebuilding a new one, while Democracy (in its more modern presentation) attempts to change society by freeing it through materialism and personal liberty. Moral intuition is the God given sense of responsibility for others, and a desire to obey God.

Each of these plans or ideologies attempt to capture men's minds and emotions through movies, music and literature. Christianity unashamedly intends to change society by first changing man through conversion to the ways of God.

In Genesis 2:17, the Lord told the man He created: "Of the tree of knowledge of good and evil, thou shalt not eat of it." Genesis 3:1-3 clearly shows Eve's sense of responsibility to obey her Creator's command. She was created with a God consciousness. I Timothy 2:14 points out that she was deceived by Satan, falling into transgression. Though deceived, the scripture still held Eve and Adam responsible for the decisions made.

Man was created with a conscience by God to discriminate between right and wrong. That this includes more than merely the "moral intuition" he possessed at creation is shown by Genesis 3:5-7, coupled with verse 22. In the first portion, Satan promises the woman that as soon as she and Adam would eat from the tree forbidden by God, their eyes would be opened and they would "be as gods, knowing good and evil."

This was not an empty promise, as confirmed by the Lord himself. In the passage, which says, "And the Lord God said, 'Behold, the man is become as one of us, to know good and evil.'" their increased knowledge in the moral realm was not merely that they had sinned, for in this they would not be like God. However, they now were able to distinguish morality objectively, from both a godly perspective and an earthly, fleshly one.

Since the fall of man, these two qualities – moral intuition and conscience became identical. The blending of the two into one quality took place before the first child was born, so that all children born into the world possess this full capability.[2]

Ancient systems of general ethics were developed before the birth of Christ. Ancient Israel wrote a negative approach to the Golden Rule. "Do not do unto others what you would not like done

---

[2] Springer, A.J. Practical Christian Living, pp. 18-19

to yourself," (negative viewpoint). This teaching falls short of Christ's teaching where He states, "Therefore all things you would that men should do to you, do so to them." This law is a summary of the ethical teaching of the law and the prophets, along with you shall love your God and your neighbor.

Confucius

Confucius became the source of one of the oldest and most important Chinese religious traditions, Confucianism. His teaching provided a strong moral code for Chinese thought and though its roots are still seen in modern Chinese belief, Communism under Mao superceded the moral code of Confucianism.

Under Confucianism, a religious movement developed by combining ancestor worship with the worship of heaven, and belief in two principles of nature called "Yin" (evil) and "Yang" (good). This movement ranks with Taoism and Buddhism among the "great" religious-ethical systems of China and other nations in Asia.

Confucius made no claim to divinity or supernatural knowledge. Neither, as we will see did Buddha, Mohammed, or other lesser teachers. Only Jesus Christ claimed to be the Son of the living God, (John 14:7). Jesus, having a theological discussion with a woman at a well, proclaims clearly that He was the Christ, the anointed one of God, (John 4:25-26).

Jesus said, "If you had known me, you should have known my Father also" (John 8:19); "I and the Father are one" (John 10:30); "Believe that the Father is in me, and I in Him" (John 14:11). Thomas, echoing bravely the thought of his contemporaries, finally believed and said, "My Lord and My God." Like Thomas, God has provided for all people the joyous privilege of knowing the one and only true God, through knowing His only begotten Son, Jesus Christ.

Confucius did not deny the existence of God; but he told his disciples he knew very little about such matters. He had no real understanding of death; his ideas were somewhat vague. He reasoned; how could one be expected to understand death if he did not first understand life? He primarily taught man to live with his fellowman with peace and to govern himself with self-discipline. Further, Confucius advised obedience to authority.

His theories dealt with five important human relationships. The relationship between:

(1) ruler and subject;
(2) parent and child;
(3) husband and wife;
(4) elder brother and younger brother;
(5) friend and friend.

Much of his teaching is helpful, even insightful, but falls short of the supreme ethic of God's Word.

Buddhism

Buddhism is a religion that emerged from Hinduism, with a supreme ethic of "working out your own salvation." Early Buddhism did not believe in God as a personal being who controls man, and no soul as an independent entity. The core of the religion is based on a path or a way of life, the object of which was to reach a condition of "enlightenment" called Nirvana. Nirvana is a blessed state of perfect life, where peace, harmony, and joy are attained. They believe Nirvana can only be understood through experience.

Buddhists, as with Hindus in general believe that all living things are reborn in new lives, and that all actions in this life will be compensated in the next. This belief of causation and rebirth is called "Karma" or cause and effect. The main concepts of Buddhism are contained in the "Four Noble Truths". These are:

1. There are sufferings in life.
2. Suffering is caused by ignorance.
3. Suffering ceases when ignorance is overcome.

4. "The Way" or "The Path," to overcome the causes of suffering is the <u>eight-fold path</u>.

The eight-fold path consists of:

    a. right understanding
    b. right occupation
    c. right thoughts
    d. right effort
    e. right speech
    f. right mindfulness
    g. right conduct
    h. right meditation

The symbol of Buddhism is a wheel with eight spokes symbolizing the Eight-Fold Path or the "Middle Way." People were to avoid extremes of following sensuous pleasures on the one hand and self-punishment on the other. The Buddhist must at all times observe high moral principles, similar to those taught by Jesus.

As stated previously, moral principles are important, and many philosophies and world religions contain wonderful teachings. But to know life requires a relationship with God through His Son, Jesus Christ.

Greek Philosophy: Sophists

The word Sophists is derived from the Greek word for wisdom. During the 4th and 5th Century B.C., the Greek pagans in the West were the first to develop a system of philosophy for life. Some of the key philosophers and their beliefs are presented here.

Protagoras (481 B.C.) was the first and the greatest of the Sophists' teachers. He was an originator of grammar; he gave us the parts of speech, the tenses and moods. He taught the belief that, "Man is the measure of all things," for he was skeptical of religion and the gods. In light of his knowledge of the importance of the

Greek/Roman gods, one can understand his prejudice. God says He, not man, is the measure of all things! "For I am God, and there is none else," and "unto me shall every knee bow, every tongue shall swear." (See: Jer. 17:5 and; Isa. 45:22-24). Jesus exclaimed, "I am the Alpha and Omega, the beginning and the end, the first and the last," (Rev. 22:13).

A second Sophist philosopher was Hippias. He taught that the permanent element in morality is, "the underlying principle of justice." His premise was not new, and was mostly incomplete, as morality was based upon the appeasement of the god's and the benefit of man on earth. This falls short of God's Word and what Israel taught 1000 years earlier.

In Deut. 10:12, Moses wrote, "And now, Israel, what does the Lord your God require of you, but to fear the Lord your God, to walk in all his ways, and to love him, and to serve the Lord your God with all your heart (mind) and with all your soul," (emotions, personality). This will be highlighted later in Chapter 6.

Micah, 200 years before Hippias wrote, "He has shown you, O man, what is good; and what the Lord requires of you, but to do justly, and to love mercy and to walk humbly with you God." Our duty to God is justice, mercy and humility. (Again, this will be expanded in Chapter 5).

The Greek philosopher Thrasymachus taught that the permanent element in morality is, "the interest of the strongest." Another way of saying this is, "might makes right!" This doctrine, often adopted by Western culture is unchristian and unscriptural. God's Word says, "We then that are strong ought to bear the infirmities of the weak, and not to please ourselves," (Rom. 15:1).

Socrates (Fifth Century) is considered the earliest and most influential of the Greek philosophers, whose ideas are known through his students Plato and Xenophon. Socrates was opposed to the Sophists teaching, placing his emphasis on logic rather than argumentation. He developed the Socratic Method of reasoning, which led his students through an argument by carefully chosen questions. He allowed them to discover their own errors and thus the answers to their own problems. Jesus also used this method, but he did it with love, not "Socratic Irony." The motto of Socrates was, "Know Yourself"; knowledge is virtue and ignorance is the only evil. "No man," he said, "willingly chooses evil (ignorance)."

Of course, Paul the apostle stated that sin is natural, easy and diabolical. The spirit is willing but the flesh is weak. With the flesh man serves sin, (Rom. 7:15-25). Paul also said that there is a battle between the flesh and the spirit, but we are to have a renewed mind, the mind of Christ, (Rom. 12:1-2). Those who are just before God are those that hear God's Word and obey it. "If you know these things, happy are you if you do them."

Socrates said, "Know Yourself," but Jeremiah 17:9-10 says, "The heart is deceitful above all things, desperately wicked: who can know it? I the Lord search the heart, I try the thoughts..."

Plato was a pupil of Socrates. He stated, "God is the highest good." This is practically the same truth as Deut. 6:5 and Mt. 22:37, (the first and greatest commandment in the law of Moses and the prophets and quoted by Christ Himself). Plato also taught that man's aim should be to know God and commune with Him, to be as nearly like Him as possible.

As noble as Plato's ideas were, God says man's wisdom cannot know God, (I Cor. 1:21). Unregenerate man cannot be like God outside of Christ. Plato, who lived before Christ, was close to the kingdom. He taught that virtue consists of wisdom, courage, moderation and justice. Of course, these are excellent qualities, though incomplete.

In Platonism, there is a general disdain for knowledge gained through the senses, relying entirely on dialogue and discussion. Plato theorized that the soul was our thoughts and the body was a hindrance to acquiring knowledge. Sight, hearing and other senses are not accurate witnesses to reality. True knowledge is revealed not to the senses but to the soul - that is to thought, in communion with the One, the universal Spirit. (Platinus Theory, 3rd Century.)

Justinian, the Emperor of the Roman Empire in 529 A.D. closed Plato's school, "The Academy of Athens." Later, when the Roman Empire weakened, Neo-Platonism became a popular religion and a rival for Christianity.

St. Augustine, one of the early fathers of the Christian Church attempted to mix concepts of Neo-Platonism with Christianity, with equally mixed results.

Aristotle was a philosopher and scientist, also a pupil of Plato, who possessed one of the greatest minds of all history. Aristotle taught that happiness is the highest good while Plato taught that, "God is the highest good." God says He has shown us what is good. We are to love the Lord our God, (Lev. 19:18), and love our neighbors as ourselves.

In the 14th Century the Catholic Church adopted Plato as an authority, infallible and unchangeable. However, experiments in science later proved many of his ideas in natural science were not true.

Aristotle and Plato taught that man's highest purpose is to imitate the action of the ultimate "Unmoved mover," God, whose only action is contemplation. Many theologians would concur with this concept in theory, yet in practice, all believe that God is not a passive observer in life on earth, but active on behalf of His children. Finally, another teaching of Aristotle was... "death is the greatest of all evils, for it is the end." Of course, we know that death is not the end, (I Cor. 15:26) for the believer or unbeliever.

The Stoics were Greek and Roman philosophers who taught that one must subdue ones feelings and thoughts in order for the mind to successfully probe the way of nature. The self-controlled, self-disciplined doctrines of the Stoics attracted Seneca and Marcus Aurelius. They believed that everything that happened to them was God's will and they must accept their lot and adapt themselves to the laws of nature. The law of nature, based upon the divine and reasonable order of the world is the basis for all man's conduct. They believed that to conform to the Word of God (which is the law of nature), was the highest goal of man. Their concept of a wise, virtuous man was one who strove to control all feelings and emotions in order to attain an acceptance of and conformity to the universal, reasonable law of nature. One should be indifferent to all outward things, finding the good entirely within ones own character. By mastering passions and emotions, one overcomes the influences of the world. This doctrine of "virtue for virtue's sake," led to an indifference to pain and pleasure. It removed the concept of a personal God; only nature as god.

"The Stoic concept of nature combined the theory of celestial fire, or a divine principle pervading all matter, with the doctrine of 'Logos,' or world reason," This left a "life according to nature."[3]

The scriptures state that the Gentiles are the "Children of disobedience" and "by nature the children of wrath," (Eph. 2:1-3). God says, "All things work out for the good to them that love God and who are called according to his purposes," (Rom. 8:28). "Also rejoice and give thanks in all things for this is the perfect will of Christ Jesus concerning you," (I Thess. 5:18).

Hedonism (circa 300 B.C.) was a philosophy divided into two schools, the Cyreniacs and the Epicureans. They believed in pleasure-seeking, personal pleasure being the height of all that is. Epicurus taught the chief good, pleasure, would bring tranquility of mind, freedom from want and pain. These could only come through self-control and simplicity of life; a similar philosophy taught in communal living. The Epicureans, along with the Stoics are mentioned in Acts 17:18. 3. In most ways, Solomon adopted the Hedonistic lifestyle, his ultimate downfall, (see Eccl.).

Concluding Thoughts

One might wonder what all of the above has to do with what God wants. Well indeed we will get there. Sometimes it is important to know what competing philosophies might be faced in the world we live in, forces that can take us far away from knowing and doing what God wants. These philosophies, many ancient and some remaining are still influential today. To know what God Wants, we must also be aware of what he *does not* want for us as His people.

---

[3]New Standard Encyclopedia P. 459

Chapter 3

Modern Systems of Ethics

Since the Protestant Reformation there have emerged several ethical (moral) systems of thought. They are briefly discussed here.

Evolutionism

Social evolution is somewhat based upon concepts found in the theory of organic evolution, but emphasizes a system of ethics based upon the theory of evolution. If man evolved from primates, then he, through an evolutionary process of learning (experiences), now has the knowledge of what is harmful to society. Those things that are harmful, including lying, stealing, etc., are to be avoided, and those things that are helpful, such as truth and honesty are to be embraced. The harmful things are wrong and the helpful things are right. Unfortunately, who decides what is harmful and helpful, truthful or dishonest is open to debate.

The Bible clearly states what is right and wrong in the Ten Commandments and other moral teachings of Scripture. (Rom. 5:12-22). With the law, people knew what behaviors were sinful. Gods' requirements are declared by Him throughout Scripture. "The Lord God commanded the man saying..." (Gen. 2:16-17). "Thou shalt..." Thou shalt not..." (Ex. 20:1-4). In the Sermon on the Mount, Jesus Christ continually repeats with emphasis, "I say unto you...This is my commandment...You are my friends, if you do what I command you." (Mt. 5:1 & John 15:10-14).

Utilitarianism

Another system of thought/ethics is Utilitarianism. To do what is useful and needful, apart from what is right and wrong, leads to what is right. Simply put, if an action is beneficial, it is right, if not, it is wrong. The chief good is "the greatest happiness of the greatest number." Benjamin Franklin's statement, "Honesty is the best policy" is an expression of utilitarianism. Thus, honesty is not a duty toward God or man; but it is the best policy for society as a whole. This doctrine of doing what is needful would bring about the theory of "any means to a desirable end," which is a Machiavellian concept akin to "The end justifies the means." "Let us do evil that good may come" is condemned by Paul (Rom. 3:5-8).

A third modern theory is that of placing right in the hands of Civil Authority: Whatever the state or government commands is right; what it forbids is wrong. Nazism and Fascism of World War II, where men gave blind obedience to their government setting aside God's laws, is a supreme example of this philosophy. Scripture states, "Render therefore unto Caesar the things which are Caesar's; and unto God the things that are God's," (Mt. 22:21).

In case of conflict, which takes precedence over the other? Acts 5:29 states, "We ought to obey God rather than men." We are commanded to obey the state because it was set up as an authority over us by God, (Rom. 13:1-7; I Pet. 2:13-17). Of course, obedience to God comes first when the command runs counter to God's commandment, (see Daniel 3:17-18).

Individualism

The individual does whatever he feels, whatever will gratify or bring him the greatest satisfaction. Thus, self-gratification: eat, drink, and be merry, tomorrow you may do it again was the belief. Much of what is seen in materialistic Western Culture, driven by media, is a picture of this philosophy of life gone wild. Even in the church we see an exaltation of the individual above the group, which is antithetical to the Biblical record.

We must remember that, "For none of us lives to himself, and no man dies to himself. For whether we live, we live unto the Lord; and whether we die, we die unto the Lord: whether we live therefore, or die, we are the Lord's," (Rom. 14:7-8 2). Further, Paul states, "But when you sin so against your brothers, and wound their weak conscience, you sin against Christ. Wherefore, if eating meat offends my brother, I will eat no flesh while the world remains, lest I hurt my brother," (I Cor. 8:12-13). We must keep our individualism (even salvation) balanced with our responsibility to others.

Altruism

Altruism is the belief that the interests of others should control one's conduct. If a cake were cut and passed, Johnny would take the smallest piece, preferring his brother and sister first. Certainly, altruism is preferable to individualism, though neither are sufficient to bring us into the fullness of What God wants.

"Then one of them, which was a lawyer, asked him a question, tempting him, saying, Master, which is the great commandment in the law? Jesus said to him, You shall love the Lord your God with all your heart, and with all your soul, and with all your mind. This is the first and great commandment. And the second is like unto it, You shall love your neighbor as yourself. On these two commandments hang all the law and the prophets," (Mt. 22:35-40).

Final Thoughts

No philosophy or religion, ancient or modern is sufficient to satisfy a Christian wanting to serve the Lord. The bible speaks to what is required of those who really desire to live the Christian life to its fullest. Thus, we will now begin to explore what God wants based upon the Word of God.

Chapter 4

The Bible as the Basis for Christian Ethics

The Bible is the Word of God; God-breathed and inspired. The importance of studying God's Word is emphasized in Scripture. "All Scripture is given by inspiration of God; and is profitable for doctrine, for reproof, for correction, for instruction in righteousness: that the man of God may be perfect, thoroughly furnished unto all good works," (I Tim. 3:16).

Further, David stated that the law of the Lord is perfect converting the soul, and Apostle Peter proclaimed that the Word is, "Able to give wisdom unto salvation," (I Pet. 1:23). Though the conscience of man is bent towards ethics, the conscience may have defects: we can't depend upon it completely. For many their conscience may be ignorant, (Acts 23:1; Acts 26:9), disabled by lack of usage. It may be defiled, (Tit. 1:15 3), by sin or unbelief, or even seared, (I Tim. 4:2).

Seared means "to render callous or insensible," by continued disobedience, or holding on to traditions of men, rather than embracing truth. Reasoning out an action frequently is the cause of sin. We cannot depend upon reason alone for Christian ethics; but only the Word of God. Eve sinned by reasoning, "she saw that the tree was good for food," (Gen. 3:6 2. Gen. 1:27).

We must remember that we were created in God's image; so we were created with intelligence and reason before the fall. However, our ability to reason after the fall has been tainted, leading many to err. For example, Cain used his reasoning when he brought God an offering that he thought was good enough. His heart motivation was immediately discerned by the Lord as suspect. He knew the requirements of God to bring his very best. He reasoned for less, the results being a seared conscience, and a depressed mood, (see Gen. 4). Cain also reasoned that he needed to kill Abel to get expunged of his jealousy.

David reasoned how to rid himself of Uriah. First, David would make Uriah think the baby was his own by calling Uriah from the battlefield, encouraging him to have relations with his wife to cover his sin. Second, he would put Uriah in the forefront of the battle. He even used his leaders to arrange his final death. His "reasoning" flowed from a guilty conscience.

New Testament Understandings

The nation of Israel had "a zeal for God," but not "according to knowledge;" they were "ignorant of God's righteousness," and were "attempting to establish their own righteousness," (Rom. 10:1-3).

The Sadducees were guilty of false reasoning in the doctrine of the resurrection of the dead. Two reasons are given for this. First, they were ignorant of the scriptures, secondly, they were ignorant of the power of God, (Mt. 22:29-32). Unbelievers are often mistaken in their reasoning, as they are deceived by Satan himself, (II Cor. 4:4; Mt. 24:5, 11) or by wicked men.

Paul says his reason did not give him a perfect knowledge of the truth, (I Cor. 13:12) or even a perfect knowledge of what to pray for, (Rom. 8:26). Since natural reasoning is so limited, what are we to do? Thankfully, we have the mind of Christ, so we can use our sanctified reason to fulfill Godly purpose. The Word of God states that by reason we receive faith and understanding, (Rom. 10:17; Mt. 13:23). In essence, we are to be converted so we can use our conscience properly. Then we are to apply the Word to our lives, mixed with faith, believing God's perfect grace toward us. But, we are not to know God's Word intellectually alone, but we are to do the Word to be called a lover of God.

Of Great Value

What value is there in applying God's Word to our lives? We please and glorify God in believing the Word He has spoken.

Further, the performance of good works pleases God, giving Him glory. Paul admonished Titus, his son in the Lord to, "Maintain good works," (Tit. 3:8, 14) and be "zealous of good works," even establish a "pattern of good works," (Tit. 2:7, 14). Thus, when others see our good works, it causes them to glorify God, (Mt. 5:16; I Pet. 2:12) which is our highest call. We are to labor, as chosen men and women of God, having been accepted by God, we are honored to please him by our works motivated by love.

"For we must all appear before the judgment seat of Christ; that everyone may receive the things done in his body, according to that he hath done whether it be good or bad. ...knowing therefore the terror of the Lord, we persuade men...made manifest in your consciences," (II Cor. 5:9-11).

Paul further wrote, "Do you not know that your body is the temple of the Holy Ghost? ...For you are bought with a price: therefore glorify God in your body," (I Cor. 6:19-20). Our acceptable service to God is to yield our bodies as a living sacrifice which is well pleasing to him, (Rom. 12:1-2). Our service to God is to show others (believers) a pattern of good works for them to follow, (Tit. 2:6-8). We are to "walk in truth," so that we can cause those who care for us and watch out for our souls to rejoice because of or positive example. (II John 3,4). We are to win unbelievers by our example of behavior even more than our words, (I Cor. 7:16, wives see I Pet. 3:1, 2).

We apply God's Word to our lives, since we have been blessed: We are blessed with "the peace of God, which passes all understanding, shall keep "our" hearts and minds through Christ Jesus," (Phil. 4:5-9). Also, we are blessed with the fellowship with God, (I Jn. 1:3-7). Remember, if we walk in the light we have fellowship with God; if not we walk in darkness. It is exciting to know we are blessed with His joy; Of course, obedience brings joy, (Jn. 15:10-11).

Finally, we are blessed with future rewards and inheritance: We all have to appear at the judgment seat of Christ. The test of our good works or service whether it is hay, wood or stubble, or gold, silver, and precious stones will be revealed at Christ's appearing. Thus, it is imperative that we live, not through a works mentality, but by the marvelous grace of God, pleasing the Lord in all we say and do.

Old Testament Ethics

There are three different eras covering 4000 years, each must be carefully distinguished in order to understand the ethics of the Old Testament.

The first era is between Creation and the Fall, were God gave Adam one negative moral commandment. "Of the tree of the knowledge of good and evil, thou shall not eat of it." It was a simple commandment, requiring simple obedience and no forethought. It should have been an easy one to keep; for this was the only tree from which he could not eat. It was simple but very important; man would surely die if he disobeyed.

Satan "the old serpent" (Rev. 12:9) tempted Eve. It is rather strange that Adam, being "perfect," allowed him in the garden. Eve was deceived, (I Tim. 2:14). She knew she was disobeying God, but her human reasoning saw a "good evil," and through eating the fruit would gain an advantage for herself and her husband. Adam deliberately sinned, he was not deceived. He willfully disobeyed and knew the end result of that sin. If Adam did not follow Eve in the disobedience he would lose fellowship with his wife. He chose between God and Eve; he was guilty of deliberate disobedience to God, (Gen. 3:1-6), and all mankind suffered because of his decision.

The second era is between the Fall and Sinai (the giving of the law). After the Fall, man became "like God... to know good and evil," (Gen. 3:22). He could now discern between right and wrong, good and evil. His inner voice or conscience guided him (or at least should). But their conscience didn't prevent them from continuing to sin, nor did it rid them of sin or guilt. Adam and Eve's son Abel evidently knew that animal sacrifice and the shedding of blood was necessary to cover sin, after his parents sinned, for God put "coats of skin" on them, (Gen. 3:21). This is the first time an animal was sacrificed for sin; to cover. This sacrifice covered their sin and allowed God to have some fellowship with Adam and Eve.

Abel, by his conscience knew he needed an animal sacrifice to put him in a right relationship with God. His sacrifice, (the firstlings of his flock) demonstrated recognition of his sin, a repentant heart, and faith that God would restore him through the death of a substitute. Cain also knew this, but he brought "the first of the ground," the efforts of his hard labor; "good works" before God as a substitute for his sins. He expected God to bless his offering: but, as previously stated, God knew his heart. God did not receive his offering since it was but an offering, not a first-fruit of a sincere, repentant heart. Cain knew what was right as far as sacrifice. Of course, the result of Cain's disobedience was an internalization of guilt and shame, and a subsequent projection of blame onto his brother Abel. Yet, though the sin (anger leading to murder) was "at the door" of his heart, he still had the ability to choose to do right…he chose to act out his rage and murdered his brother.

There are examples in Scripture where the righteous man feared God and walked with a perfect[4] heart towards Him.

For example, Enoch, "walked with God," (Gen. 5:22, 24). Noah, "was a just man and perfect, and he… walked with God," (Gen. 6:9). They were perfect in a sense that they feared God and had an honest heart. They wanted and worked to obey all of God's commandments. Yet all men on earth were corrupt and violent, which grieved God's heart, (Gen. 6:9).

With Noah, God established a covenant, (Gen. 6:18). The only commandment of God was to, "Make an ark…" and to take living creatures aboard with his family (Gen. 6:14). (Part of this covenant is salvation.) Noah obeyed all that God commanded, (Gen. 6:22;

---

[4] This does not mean sinless, but having a desire to follow God.

7:5). After the flood, Noah built an altar, (Gen. 9:20) and offered the correct sacrifice, thus God made His covenant with Noah.

One of the greatest examples of faith, covenant and right moral conduct can be seen in the life of Abraham, "who believed in the Lord; and he counted it to him for righteousness," (Gen. 15:6). God made a 7-fold covenant with Abraham with part of it to be unfolded throughout what remains of history. The Lord commanded Abram to leave his country, his father's people, and go to a land God would show him. If he obeyed, God said he would:

1. Make of him a great nation.
2. Make his name great.
3. Be a blessing to all families of the earth.

After Abram separated from Lot (whom he foolishly took with him, against God's command), God gave him a vision and a promise, (Gen. 13:9 & 15-18). He would make his seed as the dust of the earth so they can't be numbered. His only commandment was for Abram to arise and walk through the whole land. Abram obeyed, and he removed his tent and started living in the land. He built an altar in Hebron. (The same place David set up his Kingdom.)

In Time, Abraham would be called upon to fight, where he defeated the three kings, and offers a tithe to Melchizedek (a type of Jesus Christ, who first presented him the bread and wine of communion) of all the spoil taken in the rescue of Lot. (Gen. 14:16; 15:18-20). At this time, there was no Levitical priesthood. Thus, this is a picture of the priesthood of Christ, a greater priesthood (Heb.). Because of Abraham's obedience, God cuts covenant with Abraham so he knows he shall inherit the land of Canaan. For the first time, God lays down a command of a proper sacrifice (Gen. 15:9).[5]

---

[5] For more on Blood Covenant, See Denis Plant's book "Blood Covenant".

God's first ethical commandment states, "I am the Almighty God; walk before me, and be perfect." He changes his name to Abraham, which means a "father of many nations," (Gen. 17:1-6). God's everlasting covenant would be established through Abraham's seed, whose seed we are, (Gal. 3:14, 16-29). He would be their God forever, (Gen. 17:7-8) and they would have an everlasting possession. The only stipulation was that they also must keep the covenant. As a token of this covenant, they were to circumcise every male 8 days old, and every man including the stranger bought with money, (Gen. 17:9-14). Scripture also states "Command your children and your household to keep the way of the Lord, to do justice and judgment," (Gen. 18:19). Further, an angel told Abraham, "I know that thou fear God," (Gen. 22:12, 17-18) a statement of the heart of the prophet of God. Because Abraham obeyed God's voice in not withholding his only son from sacrifice; God gave his blessing. Thus, James calls Abraham "a friend of God," (James 2:23). Ultimately, the fulfillment of God's covenant with Abraham has occurred in Christ.

Sadly, the vast majority of men from Adam to Moses were wicked, as the depths of the thoughts of their hearts were evil continually, (Gen. 6:5).

The results of evil were iniquity in the heart, such as was manifested in Cain's murder of his brother, (Gen. 4:8). Lamech, of the lineage of Cain killed a man, (Gen. 4:23). In the days of Noah the earth was filled with violence, (Gen. 6:12-13). By the time of Abraham all men had become idolaters, (Joshua 24:14-15).

Further, they served other gods in Egypt for 400 years. Even after God's great deliverance and divine provision, they served other gods in Canaan Land. There are other examples, to include, "Rachel had stolen the images that were her father's," (The household gods) (Gen. 31:19). Laban was an idolater, worshipping images. Rachel also worshipped them or at least thought they would bring her "good luck" after 13 years of marriage to Jacob.

The Lord told Abraham that the "iniquity of the Amorites was not yet full," (Gen. 15:16). This iniquity was permitted another 400 years, until God allowed them to be utterly destroyed, (Deut. 20:17-18). The sin of Sodom and Gomorrah was great and their sin grievous. God could not find more than four righteous people in the whole city. Just how great was the righteousness of the four? Lot's wife looked back, indicating her heart was in the world, acting contrary to the Word of God. As we know, Lot's wife was consumed, being turned into a pillar of salt.

In Lot's day, even the greatest of sin was common, as seen when Lot's daughters committing incest with their father, having made him drunk. Further, they chose selfishly "all the plain of Jordan," (Gen. 13). Then he pitched his tent toward Sodom; later we find him living in Sodom. He sat "in the gate of Sodom" meaning he helped to rule it as a civil authority. The city was full of homosexuals who desired "to know" his visitors (angels). He offers his two virgin daughters for immoral purposes instead of having faith in God. The angels could have withstood the men of the city and utterly destroyed the whole city.

Yet, II Peter 2:7 says: he was a just man, "vexed with the filthy conversation (conduct) of the wicked," but Lot found grace and mercy and God saved his life, (Genesis 19:19). Men who lived during this time had very little to guide them except their consciences and dreams, (Gen. 20:3). With a few exceptions they were exceedingly sinful. God held them accountable for: failure to walk with God and to obey his voice and failure to bring the sacrifices required by the Lord.

No matter how "perfect" Old Testament saints were, the Bible says, "all have sinned and have fallen short of the glory of God." All have gone astray. Sarah proposed that Abraham obtain his heir by having relations with her servant Hagar. Abraham and Isaac both lied about their wives for fear of being killed, (Gen. 20:2). God had said, "through Isaac he would establish his everlasting covenant and with his seed after him," (Gen. 17:19). How merciful God was and is, as He used grossly sinful people to fulfill His covenant purposes though.

To fulfill the first part of Abraham's covenant, God raised up

Moses to lead the people out of Egypt into Canaan Land. They were to be a Chosen People, separated to God; called by God to be a Kingdom of Priests. But they were afraid to listen to God's voice, or to deal with God directly, so Moses was chosen as their intercessor, and Aaron became his spokesman or priest. God gave the moral and civil law through Moses, which was to be their guide until the seed (Abraham's) was raised up, which is Christ, (Gal. 3:16).

The Law of Moses was given only to Israel, (Ex. 19:3-6). This did not do away with the need for conscience. The moral law, fulfilled in Christ, was an external standard for ethical behavior. Yet, as the prophets spoke the laws of God (His moral conscience, the mind of Christ), were to be written on their heart.

The law of Moses added to their conscience, instructing them how to live, and showing them their sin, (Rom. 3:19-20). God knew that people could never "walk with God" in good conduct until a right relationship was established with Him. This relationship can come only through an acceptable, proper sacrifice. This is why God always put a right sacrifice at the top of his list of obedience. God knew man's reasoning, so he left nothing to chance or popular opinion. He prescribed the type of sacrifices required in detailed directions, as a shadow of the sacrifice to come, namely Christ.

Further, He prescribed a priesthood to offer these sacrifices through. It couldn't be just anyone who gave sacrifice for the people. The sons of Aaron of the tribe of Levi, and only the head of the family were the high priest to bring atonement for Israel's sins. Even then the priests failed in leadership, causing the people to sin. Before the people had a chance to receive the law, they, under the leadership of Aaron, made and worshipped the golden calf, (Exodus 32:1-6, 19). Less than a generation later, the people were guilty of wholesale idolatry, (Numbers 25:1-3).

Aaron made the golden calf pretending it was a type of worship to the Lord, (Exodus 32). He said, "Tomorrow is a feast to the Lord." His sons Nadab and Abihu offered, "strange fire before the

Lord, which he commanded them not to do." They tried to step into the High Priest's job, a most serious offense; they died in the process, (Lev. 10:1-2).

The story of iniquity and unethical conduct was most fully seen in Eli's sons. They were of "Belial" and they didn't know the Lord, (I Sam. 2:12). They even committed fornication in the temple. In Isaiah's day, the priests were erring in vision and drunkenness, (Isa. 28:7-8).

The priests in the days of Hezekiah had not kept the Passover, (II Chron. 30:5). Josiah's priest found the book of the law and he knew God's displeasure. The Passover had not been kept every year as prescribed in the law, (II Kings 22:13). Proper conduct comes with the right sacrifice. All through Israel's history they made improper sacrifice. Therefore their conduct was also improper, disapproved and judged by God.

Further examples can be seen in the wilderness where Israel complained, murmured and wept against God, coupled with unbelief. Because of this they could not enter the Promised Land; the penalty for their iniquity was death, (Num. 14:26-30; Heb. 3:17-19; I Cor. 10). The next generation committed "whoredom with the daughters of Moab," (Num. 25:1).

In the book of Judges "Every man did that which was right in his own eyes." This summarizes the condition of the heart of so many, not just then but now. In the book of Judges we see an unfortunate cycle. Their pattern for over 200 years was, to do evil in the sight of the Lord. They were sold into bondage and then they repented.

Once they repented, the Lord raised up a judge to deliver them. In spite of this well-known pattern, the children of Israel were ultimately sold into captivity. The reason the 10 tribes went into captivity in Assyria (II Kings 17:16-17) was because "they left all the commandments of the Lord their God... and they caused their sons and their daughters to pass through the fire; and used divinations and enchantments and sold themselves to do evil in the sight of the Lord, to provoke him to anger."

Isaiah wrote his nation was sinful, "a people laden with iniquity..." evildoers. They served other gods after returning from the Babylonian captivity. They polluted the bread, sacrificed the blind, the lame, and sick, (Mal. 1:7-8). In Jesus' day, at the very end of the era of the law, even the high priests erred. They mocked Jesus at the foot of the cross.

Some Criticisms of Old Testament Ethics

There was much we can learn from the ethical standards and lapses found in the Old Testament. Old Testament ethics are substandard to the ethics of the New Testament. Some have asked, "Did God change from the Old Testament times to the New? Is He the same God?"

One thing is certain, God is "from everlasting to everlasting," (Ps. 90:2). The Lord is unchanging, unaffected by circumstances, immutable, (Mal. 3:6) "I am the Lord, I change not." (see Heb. 13:8) God is perfect from the beginning and perfection cannot be improved upon. "The counsel of the Lord stands forever, the thoughts of his heart to all generations," (Ps. 33:11).

Has the concept of God changed from the Old Testament to the New? We only know from the Bible what God desires to reveal about Himself; what man conceives is not always true. God reveals the things of himself by His Spirit. We see that, "The world by wisdom knew not God," (I Cor. 1:21). The natural man does not receive the things of the Spirit of God, (I Cor. 2:10-14). The Old Testament reveals the same thing, (Deut. 29:29). The emphasis in the Old Testament is on his justice, in the New, on His grace. Calvary is the reason.

We don't have one God in the Old and one God in the New; but what we know about God has changed. First, man was innocent. After the fall he knew the difference between good and evil. Finally under the Law, and because of the Law, Israel knew much more about God, his nature, and his standards (and as seen in the teachings of Paul, revealed our sin). Under grace, far more has been revealed to us about God. We are now given the ability through grace to keep His standards.

Jesus' Sermon on the Mount furnished the most disciplined teaching on ethics in all literature. "He made known unto us the "mystery of His will," (Eph. 1:9). "Be perfect, even as your Father which is in heaven is perfect," (Mt. 5:48). His will from the beginning has not change, as he revealed to our Father Abraham; "I am the Almighty God' walk before me, and be perfect."

Other Examples

Polygamy

Solomon had many wives; his downfall was "strange women" and the idols they worshipped. Abraham had two wives: Sarah and Keturah, but only one at a time, and had a child by Hagar, his concubine. Isaac, the Son of the Promise, had only one; Rebekah. Jacob had four wives: Rachael, Leah, Bilhah, Zilpah. David had seven wives: (II Sam. 3:2-5, 14; 5:13).

Multiple marriage was never commanded by God, nor was it ever approved by Him. By implication, it was forbidden by God. "Therefore, shall a man leave his father and his mother, and shall cleave unto his wife: (not wives) and they shall be one flesh," (Gen. 2:24). God made "a help meet" for man. The noun is singular. "The two shall become one flesh," (Mt. 19:5).

Lying

The best of God's people have it recorded forever that they have lied. Lying is a sin; yet we rarely see where God immediately pointed a finger at their sin and punished them. Under the Old Covenant, God judged the people by their outward actions; i.e.: Did their conversation or action bring grief and hurt to others? This is in sharp contrast to the New Covenant where people are judged by their thoughts, intents, and motives as well as their actions, (Mt.

5:17-20, 27-28, 31-34. 4).

It is in Job 13:4, that we find the earliest recording of the evil of lying: "But you are forgers of lies, you are all physicians of no value." Proverbs 12:18 finishes the thought, "but the tongue of the wise is health." David spoke against lying in Psalm 31:18, "Let the lying lips be put to silence, which speak grievous things proudly and contemptuously against the righteous. Remove from me the way of lying, (Ps. 119:29). I hate and abhor lying, (Ps. 119:163).

David repented from lying. He stated in Psalm 120:2, "Deliver my soul, O Lord, from lying lips and a deceitful tongue." Solomon, the wisest man in history, wrote about lying lips, (Prov. 10:18; 14:5, 25; 19:5, 9; 30:8). "A lying tongue is but for a moment... Lying lips are an abomination to the Lord," (Prov. 12:19, 22). "All the earth sought to Solomon to hear his wisdom which God had put in his heart," (I Kings 10:24). Yet... "his heart was not perfect with the Lord his God as was the heart of David his father," (I Kings 11:4).

One thousand years after David, God reveals to Isaiah: "And of whom have you been afraid or feared, that you have lied, and have not remembered me, nor laid it to your heart? Have not I held my peace even of old, and you feared me not? ...but he that puts his trust in me shall possess the land, and shall inherit my holy mountain."

God reveals more of himself; that lying is a sin against God, because we do not fear him and remember his judgments. There is also the promise of a holy inheritance to a people not yet fulfilled. God holds his peace; he permits sin to go on temporarily, in order that he may show His mercy and grace. If he didn't, the world would suddenly cease to exist, (II Pet. 3:9).

Now let's consider war. GOD NEVER DESTROYED WITHOUT REASON OR A CAUSE. "You have heard that it was said by them of old time, You shall not kill; and whosoever shall kill shall be in danger of the judgment: But I say unto you, that whosoever is angry with his brother without a cause shall be in danger of the judgment; and whosoever shall say to his brother,

Ra'-ca, shall be in danger of the council; but whosoever shall say, You fool, shall be in danger of hell fire," (Mt. 5:21-22).

This verse plus Luke 3:14 are used by dissenters of war. But this verse is speaking to Roman soldiers. They are compared to a brutal police force of today. They were actually taking bribes and falsely accusing others. This verse has no bearing to war. Jesus said render to Caesar the things that are Caesar's and to God the things that are God's, (Mt. 22:21). Several times the scripture states that civil authority and government is to be obeyed as long as it doesn't cause one to disobey God. There is no scripture which can be easily interpreted to state that one may refuse to go to war. In fact, God orders war, saying "When you got to war against your enemy..." War was to be used to withstand anything idolatrous, (Deut. 20:1). The only stipulations were that they not be afraid; the fearful were sent home. Those that had just been married could stay home, along with those that had just built a home, planted a vineyard; anyone with divided interests because they had not eaten of the fruits of their endeavors, (Deut. 20:5-8).

The concept of a "just war" has been discussed for generations, and has been hotly debated due to present geopolitical conflicts. What constitutes a just war? Oil interests? Need for more territory? Manifest destiny? As Christians, we are naturally interested in justice and mercy, care for the poor and protection for "the least of these." Balancing a national interest with Kingdom principles is not easy, but must be grappled with.

For example, in the recent Iraq war, to see a tyrant, Saddam Hussein dethroned was no doubt a good. The cost of lives, growth of church (which has been negative) has been affected greatly. Are we as Christians on the side of justice (remove terrorists, dictator, etc.) or mercy (care for the thousands of lives destroyed in the process, or both, and to what measure? These are in fact heady concerns with no easy answers.

We may be called upon, in the defense of a nation, to go to war. If a nation invades the sovereignty of another, war may be required, but must be entered into with a hope of as few casualties as possible amongst non-combatants.

Punishment that Fits the Crime

Now consider the severity of punishment found in scripture. It is important to provide an answer for people who think that God was cruel and vengeful in dealing with certain individuals or nations. These apparent edicts by God are some of the most difficult to grapple with in scripture. One must consider the type of people (barbaric) existed in that day, and consider the progressive understanding of God, his goodness and grace as you deal with these concepts.

For example, Saul was ordered to destroy every Amalekite and every living thing, including women, children and animals, (I Sam. 15:3). Because Saul refused to obey God in this matter, the kingdom was taken from him and given to David, a man after God's own heart. If kept alive the Amalekites would lead Israel astray to worship false gods. The heads of all the people were hung up before the Lord in the hot sun, (Num. 25:4). They had allowed the people to commit immorality with the daughters of Moab. The people bowed down and sacrificed to their gods; the greatest sin man can commit is to worship another god. They also committed fornication. This sin then endangered all Israel; but especially the children, (Deut. 4:1-4).

In Deut. 7:16-18, God ordered that when he delivered the enemy into their hand they were to utterly destroy all life. They were not to take pity. They were to remember what God did to Egypt, because they were exceedingly wicked. Their practices included human sacrifice, astrology, clairvoyance, dealing with evil spirits: which was forbidden by law. The penalty was death, (Deut. 18:9-14; Ex. 22:18; Lev. 20:27). God never brings judgment or punishment that he has not forewarned. He is never spiteful.

Every law breaker is forewarned what will happen to him if he defies God's authority over him and despises God's Word. Old Testament judgment was that the law breaker, in many cases, would be stoned to death by the entire congregation, (Num. 15:35). We are commanded by God to keep the Sabbath a delight. We are not to think or speak our own thoughts, nor do our own pleasure. God promised us joy, blessing, and the ability to reach spiritual heights, ecstasy in God, (Is. 58:13).

Of course, with many of the laws that state death was imminent for all law breakers, there was mitigation or lesser punishments allowed. It is important to remember that Hyperbole, or exaggeration, was often used to illustrate an important point, and many of the punishments of the Old Testament are no longer germane to today. Has God changed, no, only mans understanding of or revelation of God, made perfect through Christ.

God always, with great compassion, forewarned and gave time for the people to repent until He sent His wrath: and His wrath came only because there was (apparently) no other remedy, (II Chron. 36:15-16). God would not allow Abraham to take Canaan Land from the Amorites because the iniquity of the Amorites was not yet full, (Gen. 15:16).

In Joshua 5:1, when the Amorites heard of the crossing of the Red Sea their heart melted, there was no more spirit in them, because of the children of Israel. Remember, the Lord is not slack concerning His promise (Day of Judgment); He is not willing that any should perish, (II Pet. 3:9).

In Summary

The conduct of God and the conduct of His people are two entirely different things. God makes perfect commandments, but man's obedience is not perfect. Man may know precept upon precept as Solomon and still disobey. What people say and what they practice are often two different things. Theory or the ideal is not the actual practice in most cases. We must not forget the nature of sin which is aimed by Satan to overthrow God's government by rebellion. Further, we must remember the distinction between law and grace: Law tells us what is sinful but doesn't free the people of guilt or redeem them. Only by blood is their redemption found, by grace through Christ. "The law was given by Moses, but grace and truth came by Jesus Christ," (John 1:17).

Most important of all is the fact that in the Old Covenant God judged his people by their actions if it brought hurt to others. But in the New Covenant, men are judged by their thoughts and motives as well as their actions. Jesus said he did not come to destroy the law and the prophets, but to fulfill it (the law would stay until judgment), (Mt. 5:17-18).

Of course, our righteousness must exceed the scribes and Pharisees, (Mt. 5:20). Jesus said, under the New Covenant: one could look after a woman with the wrong motive and commit adultery, (Mt. 5:27-28 & 31-32). Any communication in verifying the truth, beyond a plain yes or no, is from the devil, (Mt. 5:33-37).

In the Old Testament: Murder required judgment. In the New Covenant, if anyone nurses anger against his brother, he is guilty of murder and faces judgment, not in this world, but in eternity. We are to love our enemies, (Mt. 5:43-48). If we forgive others of the wrongs they have done to us, then our heavenly Father will also forgive us, (Mt. 6:14-15).

Chapter 5

Bible Ethics for New Testament Christians

God cannot tolerate sin. His desire is that His people live righteously, (Is. 60:21). God cannot look upon sin: God requires natural and spiritual cleanliness in his people. It is holiness that the Lord desires, more than happiness.

From the beginning of His dealings with man, and the establishment of his Kingdom principles through Abraham, Isaac and Jacob and the giving of the Law of Moses, right relationship with God was primary. God's people were to put away strange gods from among them and be clean (symbolized by ceremonial washings and the change of garments, Gen. 3:21-23; Gen. 35:2). The Lord gave specific instructions to Moses and the children of Israel concerning uncleanness. For example, in the treating of leprosy (a type of sin) the main cure was cleanliness, (Lev. 13:6; 14:8). Also, those with an open sore were to bathe in running water and wash their clothes, (Lev. 15:4-13). All the people and the camp itself were to be kept clean and holy before the Lord.

"Thus, shall you separate the children of Israel from their uncleanliness; that they will not die... when they defile my tabernacle that is among you, (Lev. 15:31)". "A man who is unclean and does not cleanse himself shall be cut off from the midst of the assembly, (Num. 19:20-21)". The camp must be a sanctuary, especially in wartime; the enemy cannot come against a righteous camp, (Num. 23:9-12). Even the ashes of the heifer were deposited outside the camp in a clean place, (Num. 19:9).

The Levites were specifically charged and held responsible to live a clean and holy life before God and the people. The priest was to bathe himself in water before he put on holy garments, (Lev. 16:4). His garments were to be pure linen: No mixture was allowed in the priests garments, (Deut. 22:11). The Levites who served their brethren in the tabernacle were to be extra clean, (Num. 8:7, 13-16). "...Go out of the midst of her; be clean, you that carry the vessels of the Lord," (Is. 52:11).

The Pharisees were accused of making the outside of the cup clean but inwardly they were full of excess, (Mt. 23:25-28). The Pharisees fulfilled all the law of body cleanliness, in eating and washing of animals and hands. Jesus said we should exceed the Pharisees in natural and spiritual cleanliness.[6]

The Lord honors those who keep His principles of cleanliness and righteousness. He that has clean hands and a pure heart shall receive the blessing of the Lord and shall be permitted to ascend into His holy hill, (Ps. 24:3-5). "He that has clean hands shall be stronger and stronger," (Job 17:9).

When we repent from our sin, we are to turn our entire will and way over to God. Paul wrote, "...present your body as a living sacrifice unto God..., and be transformed by the renewing of your mind... (Rom. 12:1-2). Rebellion against God's way is, in His sight, the sin of witchcraft. God likens stubbornness against God's divine principles to iniquity and idolatry, (I Sam. 15:23).

It is assumed that Lucifer's sin was his failure to acknowledge God as eternally supreme and to desire to exalt himself to a position of equality with God, (Ezek. 28:15; Is. 14:13-14). He was undoubtedly filled with ambition, with a desire to ascend to a place of prominence by self-effort.

No doubt, as seen in the wilderness confrontation between Jesus and Satan, the devil desired to be served, to be worshipped, to be obeyed, to dominate. Because of his rebellious actions, he was cast out of God's presence. This same desire for self-exaltation (pride) is the chief cause of moral decline.

God's divine plan of redemption provided everything we need to live a righteous life before Him. Our responsibility as new creatures is to yield our members to Christ, (Rom. 6:11-13). We

---

[6] Of course, most of the Old Testament requirements were fulfilled in Christ, and the principles apply, if not the actual ritual. Further, much of the Old Testament requirements are commonly called types and shadows of things fulfilled in the New Testament

must put off the old nature with its deeds and put on Christ, (Col. 3:8-14).

The Christian's Duty to God in Brief

Before looking at four key aspects of What God Wants, a brief view of well known but sadly neglected duties (an easy burden, given by Christ) as believers are reviewed here.

In order to serve God in an acceptable manner our motivations must be pure. The Lord wants us to serve Him out of a pure heart of love - not out of fear, or duty, or religious conscience. Love is the first fruit of the Spirit and should be the first product in our lives, (Gal. 5:22). Love is the greatest of all Christian characteristics, (I Cor. 13:13). Love is the primary way the world knows we are Christians (or at least should), (John 13:35). Love will cast out all fear: fear of people, fear of the devil, and even an improper fear of God, (I John 4:18).

The Lord had to reprimand the church at Ephesus because they had lost their first love. The Lord's command to them was to repent and do the first work. He required an act of repentance in order to restore this first love, (Rev. 2:2-5). Once we are motivated correctly, this will affect our devotion, our obligations and our priorities; our conduct and the way we practice our service to God comes from our relationship with Him, (Col. 1:18).

Worship is Key

We have a responsibility to worship Him as Lord. Worship means: bowing in submission to the will of God, in reverence, adoration, respect, honor and devotion. We are to give the Lord glory and come before Him in worship, (I Chron. 16:29), to worship Him in the beauty of holiness, (Ps. 96:9). As David wrote, "O come let us worship and bow down," (Ps. 95:6).

God is a spirit, we are to worship Him in spirit and truth, (John 4:24). We are to worship Jesus as Lord and Christ, (John 9:38). We are to worship the Lord according to every thing that is written in the scriptures, (Acts 24:14). Our worship must not be according to our feelings or what we assume is acceptable to God, but according to the principles provided in the Word. This is real faith. By faith, Jacob, when he was dying, worshipped, (Heb. 11:21). By faith, Abraham and his sons worshipped the Lord, (Gen. 22:5, 8).

Our responsibility is to worship in community, with the congregation, (Jer. 33:11; Ps. 22:22; 35:18; 149:1). The entire congregation worshipped together bowing their faces to the ground, (II Chron. 29:28; II Chron. 7:3). We are not to worship the works of our own hands; (Mic. 5:13). The hosts of heaven; (Zeph. 1:4-5). The Queen of heaven, or the workmanship of heaven, (Jer. 44:16-19). Angels (Col. 2:18), or Devils (Rev. 9:20).

We are to remember that Jesus is the creator. He is worthy of our worship and as we worship according to His patterns He will join us in the worship, (Rev. 4:11; Rev. 5:9; Heb. 2:12).

Purposeful Prayer

Our duties and responsibilities to the Lord also include spending time with Him in open communion and prayer. Prayer will keep us from yielding to temptation, (Mt. 26:41). An effective fervent prayer will accomplish much, (James 5:16). Prayer will keep us from becoming overwhelmed with the world we live in, or becoming weary, (Luke 18:1). In prayer the Lord can reveal His will and show us things to come, (Jer. 33:3). Making our requests known to the Lord gives Him the opportunity to grant requests and bless us, (John 16:24). We should always be in an attitude of prayer, (I Thess. 5:17).

Prayer should be our first consideration in any circumstance - whether for ourselves or for others, (I Tim. 2:1). We should pray one for another and bear each others burdens, (James 5:16; Gal. 6:2). Our prayers for others should never be filled with gossip, but we should pray for people according to the scriptural pattern, (Eph. 3:14-21). Pray that they be strengthened, that their faith may increase, that they be rooted and established and fruitful in the Kingdom, that they may comprehend Christ's love and walk worthy of Him, and that they be filled with all the fullness of God and the knowledge of His will. Our prayers should always be centered on the furtherance of His kingdom, (Mt. 6:10; 9:37-38).

Dynamic Word

Consistently studying the Word is also part of our responsibility to the Lord. We cannot live up to God's standard if we don't know what it is; studying will give us this knowledge so that we can stand, approved, before God, (II Tim. 2:15). Ezra was a good example of a man who felt a responsibility toward God's Word, (Ezra 7:10).[7]

The scriptures should be studied daily, (Acts 17:11; John 5:39). "Let the word of Christ dwell in you richly in all wisdom," (Col. 3:1). Then, and only then can we fulfill the rest of the verse which is "to teach and admonish one another."

Obey

Submission and obedience will be a natural result of a proper relationship to the Lord, (Heb. 13:17). Discipline is a heavenly principle; "discipline" and "disciple" come from the same word meaning to train for orderly conduct; that which develops character, self control, orderliness and self-sufficiency, (I Sam. 15:22).

This is often the acid test for Christians; being obedient to God, (Heb. 13:7; Rom. 13:1). True obedience is from the heart and not just actions; as people see and recognize our ability to obey the Lord by obeying those in authority, they will turn and follow our example, (II Cor. 10:16).

As we climb God's ladder of authority, it is then that we will

---

[7] For more, see Keys to Successful Living by Dr. Stan DeKoven

be qualified to honor and respect the submission of others, (II Cor. 10:6). Obedience should not thwart our zeal or creativity, but channel it. We are responsible to the Lord for our attitudes. Thus, we should do all things without complaining, (Phil. 2:14-15). Our service to the church and to others must be performed as though it was a direct ministry to the Lord...because it is, (Mt. 25:40).

Our ministry before the Lord as faithful stewards is a great responsibility. God owns everything by right of creation and all things belong to Him. He is the possessor of heaven and earth, (Gen. 14:22). The earth is His and everything that dwells in it, (Deut. 10:14). The beasts of the forest and all cattle are His, (Ps. 50:10). All the silver and the gold is His, (Hag. 2:8). All riches, honor, strength and might, and glory come from Him and He reigns over it all, (I Chron. 29:11-13). All the land is His, (Lev. 25:23).

Every soul is God's, (Ezek. 18:4). We are not our own; we are bought with a price, (I Pet. 1:18-19; Mt. 23:10; I Cor. 6:20), yet, we all differ from each other, (I Cor. 4:7). He has delivered us form the powers of darkness, (Col. 1:13). He created all things, (Eph. 3:9; Gen. 1:1; Rev. 4:11).

The Lord chooses individuals in the body and gives to them a ministry, (Mt. 25:14-23). Fulfilling our responsibility in ministry gives great joy, (Mt. 25:21). Fear of displeasing people, leadership, or the Lord, often keeps us from forging ahead in what the Lord has given us to do, (Mt. 25:24-30). A steward has a great responsibility and he must be found faithful, (I Cor. 4:1-3; II Tim. 1:14).

Remember, God has entrusted us with His great message of salvation, (I Thess. 2:4; II Tim. 1:14). As an entrusted servant and steward of the gospel, our character must be above reproach, (Titus 2:7-8; I Cor. 4:2). There are different types of stewards. The good steward who manages what has been give to him or her and make it increase, (I Pet. 4:10). The wise steward, who uses wisdom in serving, (Luke 12:42). The unjust steward, who wasted both time and money, (Luke 16:1).

There are 5 cardinal points of stewardship are:

First, he/she must acknowledge that God is the owner of all things, (Gen. 14:22; Hag. 2:8). Second, as stewards we are trustees and partners of all His possessions, (Mt. 25:14; Acts 4:32). Third, we are stewards of money, time, talents and our bodies, (I Pet. 4:10). Fourth, we must acknowledge God by a separated portion, (Gen. 28:20-22; I Cor. 16:1-3). Our separated portion is the tithe, understood in a New Testament context.

A steward is accountable to God for everything entrusted to his care. The kingdom of heaven takes account of its servants, (Mt. 18:23; Rom. 14:7-12). This includes accounting to Him for our wages - our time - our expending of ourselves - what we did with the ministry given to us by the laying on of hands.

We labor to be acceptable and well pleasing to God, (Rom. 12:1; I Cor. 5:9). This does not mean we work for our salvation, but we labor because of the life given to us. Each of us must appear before the judgment seat to give an account, (II Cor. 5:10; I Cor. 4:5). To be a good steward we must be willing to forsake all to follow Christ fully. The scriptures give us clear examples of faithful or unfaithful stewards; studying these can give us the Lord's requirements for stewardship.

Stewards

In Gen. 43:19, 44:1-4, we see that the steward in Joseph's house followed his master's directions fully, even though his instructions might have seemed illogical or even cruel. But it was to be through this means that Benjamin was preserved and ultimately blessed.

David appointed faithful stewards over all the substance and possessions of the king, (I Chron. 28:1).

Elah was killed in the house of his steward, (I Kings 16:8-10).

There are wages earned and rewards received by every steward, (Mt. 20:8; Luke 12:42).

Joanna, wife of King Herod's steward ministered to Jesus from her substance, along with Mary Magdalene and other women of means, who were good stewards with generous hearts, (Luke 8:1-3).

The rich man's steward wasted his goods and was required to give an account. (Faithfulness over another man's goods is required before we can be entrusted with our own.) (Luke 16:1-13).

Thus, a steward must be blameless, (Titus 1:7).

The Lord also expects us to be good stewards of our time. Time is short. We must live and work as if the Lord were coming back tomorrow, (I Cor. 7:29). We are to redeem the time (make good use of it) and be wise, (Eph. 5:16-17; Col. 4:5). We are to be sober, vigilant, steadfast and resist Satan, (I Pet. 5:8). We are to be occupied, willingly feeding the flock of God, (I Pet. 5:2). A man should work and labor until the evening, (Ps. 104:23), with expectation of God's blessing.

If we work with our hands we will receive blessing and a sense of well being, (Ps. 128:2). He that gathers by labor shall increase, (Prov. 13:11). We are not to hate our labor, but our heart is to rejoice in all our labor, (Ecc. 2:10-18, 24). Every man will be rewarded according to his own labor, (I Cor. 3:8-9). Our good labor is not in vain in the Lord, (I Cor. 15:58). We are to work to show our faith, love, patience and hope in Jesus Christ, (I Thess. 1:3).

The scriptures give us examples of those who labored:

1) Mary worked hard, (Rom. 16:6).
2) Phebe cared for many, (Rom. 16:2).
3) Persis worked hard for the Lord, (Rom. 16:12).
4) Paul labored day and night, (I Thess. 2:9).
5) The church at Ephesus was commended for their labor, (Rev. 2:1-3).

We are to give time to the word and teaching, (I Tim. 5:17).

We are to labor for the saints of God in works of love, (Heb. 6:10). Work and stewardship are linked together throughout scripture. It is a great honor to be called as a steward of God, (Titus 1:7). We are to be good stewards who can be trusted, (I Pet. 4:10). We are commanded to be faithful and wise, (I Cor. 4:2; Luke 12:42). We are God's partners, working in His name, (III John 7).

The Lord has committed to each person a portion of His substance; we are held responsible for our time, talent and treasurer. The love of money is the root of all types of evil, (I Tim. 6:10). A Christian steward makes money, not for himself or herself alone, but to fully participate in the life of the kingdom of God, (I Tim. 6:9-12). We are not to seek money for selfish usage, but for the greater good of giving and service, (Luke 12:16-20; 16:13; 12:15). We must never make money at the price of others, (Prov. 14:31; Jer. 22:13-17).

Money making power is an endowment from God, (Deut. 8:18; Acts 14:17; Deut. 11:13-17). The basis of Christianity is found in one word "GIVE," and the Lord Himself set the example for us to follow. He gave His Son, (John 3:16). Jesus gave Himself, (Gal. 2:20). The Holy Spirit was given by the Father, through the Son, (John 14:16; 15:26).

He gives us all blessings, (James 1:27; II Pet. 1:3). His gifts are:

- Free, abundant, to be prayed for, to be used for mutual profit, to be gladly acknowledged. (Num. 14:8; Rom. 8:32; Mt. 7:7, 11; John 16:23-24; I Pet. 4:10; Ps. 4:7, 21:2.)
- His Spiritual Gifts are:

Christ, the Holy Spirit, grace, faith, righteousness, strength and power, rest, eternal life.

(Is. 42:6; John 4:10; Luke 11:13; Jas. 4:6; I Pet. 11:13; Eph. 2:8; Rom. 5:16-17; Ps. 68:35; Mt. 11:28; Rom. 6:23).

- His Temporary Gifts include:

Life, food and clothing, rain and fruitful seasons, wisdom, all good things. (Is. 42:5; Mt. 6:25-33; Gen. 27:28; Is. 30:23; II Chron. 1:12; Ps. 34:10; I Tim. 6:17).

- His Gifts Are:

Partaken of by all creatures, to be used and enjoyed, to cause us to remember Him. (Ps. 136:25; 145:15-16; Eccl. 3:13; I Tim. 4:4-5; Deut 8:18).

The collection is the touchstone of service. It is to be:

Prepared for on the first day of the week. Everyone is to cooperate in it, as we are to bring tithes and offerings, give a willing offering, donate our best toward the collection, let none come without an offering, make a freewill offering, realizing that a person cannot out give God, and what finances are collected must be managed well to fulfill the purpose of God in community. (I Cor. 16:2; I Cor. 16:2; Mal. 3:8-10; Ex. 25:2; Ex. 22:29-30; Ex. 25:15; Deut. 16:10; Ezra 1:4; Eccl. 11:1; Luke 6:38; II Cor. 8:24; I Tim. 6:18).

The Lord has designated a particular place for our tithes and offerings:

The Lord has been careful to explain how we should give and our attitudes toward giving.

We are to give without ostentation, commanded to give cheerfully, not begrudgingly, must give with liberality, make our giving systematic, giving to be proportionate to our prosperity, our giving is to be sacrificial. (Mt. 6:3; II Cor. 9:7; Prov. 11:25; I Cor. 16:2; I Cor. 16:2; II Sam. 24:24).

We are not to give out of impulse or by feelings but according to the Word. You might ask, why belabor the principles of giving. The reason is simple. One of the key demonstrations of a persons love for God is seen through their willingness to give, to give time, talent and treasurer, generously and as directed by the Holy Spirit. It is part of what God wants.

The Christians Duty to Others

As believers, we have a responsibility to maintain unity and love in the church, (Ps. 133:1-2). Paul commanded the Corinthian Church to be in unity; that there were to be no divisions, (I Cor. 1:10). Unity has always been a principle of God.

This important concept was recognized in the upper room, (Act. 1:14; 2:1). It was further recognized in the Corinthian church, (I Cor. 1:10). Jesus knew the value of this principle, and he had every expectation that unity would be achieved in him (John 17:21-22). A church or ministry that strives for unity will be one that experiences the glory of God, (Eph. 4:1-3, 13, 16; I Pet. 4:17-18). We are to unite in prayer, (Acts 1:14); in one place, (Acts 2:1; 2:46). There must be unity in God's army, (Joel 2:7-11). We are to endeavor to keep the unity of the spirit, (Eph. 4:3) in the bond of peace.

We have a responsibility to show proper respect for those in positions of authority in the Body of Christ. Five fold ministries are given to us as gifts by the Lord, (Eph. 4:11; Jer. 3:15). Leaders are shepherds of the flock and are workers with God, (Jer. 23:4). We should be careful to build up the leadership, especially apostles and prophets, to be that of "presidential importance" to our children. We should never make derogatory remarks against a spiritual leader or his/her spouse in the presence of children. They play an important role in God's program.

Children usually receive divine healing through prayer by the spiritual leader as they are taught to respect the pastor and other ministers. Children, as well as adults, show their respect to God as they respect their local leaders. Thus, it is important to encourage children and young people to learn the value and wisdom of counseling with their spiritual elders. It is a parents responsibility to provided continual instruction to children, and include in their teaching the importance of cooperating and obeying all legitimate church leadership.

We are to give our respect to the office of five fold ministry leaders and elders. God's Word says they are divinely called, (Rom. 1:1). No one just decides to be a minister. They are divinely made, (I Tim. 1:12) and God-given, (Eph. 4:11).

There are five moral qualifications given for those in the position of Elder or Five Fold Minister. They are to be blameless, having no accusation against their character. They are to demonstrated self-control, be sober in thought and deed, with good behavior, as an example to others. And they are to be patient, because it takes great patience to lead God's people.

God's Word says their ministry should be identified, recognized and is worthy of double honor, (I Tim. 5:17). Also, Deacons are worthy of our respect. They are appointed to a position of authority by the Elders, (Acts 6:3). They have specific qualifications as well. They are to be: husband of one spouse, not gossips, sober, faithful in all things. Their moral qualifications include being; straightforward in communication, not addicted or greedy of money, blameless, and with proven character and service. (I Tim. 3:8-10). Spiritual qualifications include being full of the Holy Spirit, full of wisdom, reverent, holding the mystery of faith in a pure conscience (knowing and obeying the Word).

The word deacon means servant, which gives us an understanding of their area of work. They must serve and manage their own families well, (I Tim. 3:12). They are also to minister to the body in physical labor in order to release the ministries from material duty, (Acts 6:3). Though they are not required to ministry the word of God, many are able, being strong in faith, while demonstrating a balanced ministry, (I Tim. 3:13).

We have a responsibility to show proper respect to every ministry in the church. Essentially, the scripture urges us to know one another after the spirit, not just according to personality or the status we might have in the world, (II Cor. 6:16-19).

Parents

We must also be careful to set a proper example of respect for the position of fathers, mothers and the elderly. We must never disrupt or destroy parental authority by council or by siding with a child against his parents. The parent's duty is to train a child and set the boundaries of activities and behavior. Again, we must be careful not to destroy their authority in this function.[8]

In Western society there is little reverence and respect paid to the elderly. In the body of Christ we must oppose this trend, (Lev. 19:32). The elderly need our love and attention. They need the support of the young, for they are important to the body of Christ.

Remember, someone is always watching us. Our responsibility is to build each other up but the grace of God in us, while being constantly aware that our conduct is above reproach.

This includes such practical things as: faithful attendance at church services whenever possible. We should be cordial and friendly, especially to visitors. Punctuality at all the services is a blessing to others, and demonstrates that church is a priority. Further, we should do our best to keep the church property neat and clean, and treat church supplies as sacred.

It is also wise to be an example in our appearance. We should realize that many people have different backgrounds concerning 'holiness'. We should esteem the body of Christ higher than our need for fashion. We must be especially careful not to offend the little ones (in the natural and in the spiritual).

Areas of Questionable Activities

Paul's position on his activities is the best rule to follow, (Rom. 14:20-23). In this passage, Paul summarizes in many ways the results of the message of Christ and the Kingdom. In the Kingdom of God, which is now manifested in the world through the church, there are ways of living that are acceptable to the King. Our ethic is to be a mirror reflection of the teachings, or if you will the principles of the Kingdom of God, or God's rule everywhere over

---

[8] For more on honoring and parenting, see Dr. DeKoven's *Parenting on Purpose*.

everything. The King is the Father of the citizens over which he rules. Thus, the apostolic church no doubt spent much time in teaching the moral ramifications of living under the rule of our benevolent and merciful King.

We are commanded by the Lord not to love the world system, (I John 2:15-16). Nothing we do should cause us to come into bondage, (I Cor. 10:23). With this attitude, the Lord will help us to choose those activities which will edify and build up the body of Christ, and be a witness of salt and light in the communities in which we live. Alistair McGrath states in "The Portable Seminary, page 620 " Let us think of ourselves, our seminaries, our churches, and our families as colonies of heaven, as outposts of the real eternal city, who seek to keep its laws in the midst of alien territory. C.S. Lewis gave us many helpful ways of thinking about the Christian life, and one of the most helpful is that of the world as enemy territory, territory occupied by invading forces. We must never be afraid to be different from the world around us. It is easy for Christians to be depressed by the fact that the world scorns our values and standards....and so our moral vision—grounded in Scripture sustained by faith, given intellectual spine by Christian doctrine—stands as a civilizing influence in the midst of a world that seems to have lost its moral way."

Impartiality

There are strong admonitions to believers in regards to showing partiality in church or church fellowship, (James 2:1-4). One of Peter's greatest revelations was that God was no respecter of persons, (Acts 10:34). Remember, Jesus died for all, so we are to have fellowship and show respect to all. This does not mean that you can not have personal friends. However, if one is in leadership, it's not good to have only one or two close friends in the church. In this position of responsibility, fellowship and friendship must be given to all. A clique is a small exclusive set of persons which can be very detrimental to church life. Keep busy and involved with the whole body.

All members of the body must be able to receive from every gift, and all of the fruit of the Spirit at any time, (Gal. 5:22-23). This is part of our responsibility to the body of Christ. Our first fruit (love) should be always in season, (Ps. 1:3; I Tim. 4:2).

We are also responsible to be effective personal workers in personal ministry to those in need. We should always be able to lead someone to the next step in their spiritual experience, (I Pet. 3:15). We are all called to be caregivers of others. To be an effective caregiver, it is essential to have genuine concern for people's spiritual needs and growth. This is not "natural" to many, thus men and women must be trained and qualified by their spiritual leaders. Those that care for others must first be walking victoriously, and be prepared through the word of God to provide others with a scriptural basis for spiritual growth.

Discipline

There are seven points of unity in discipline. Sin is everyone's responsibility. When sin is seen in a brother or sister, it is our responsibility to confront them in love, with a spirit of meekness and attitude of restoration, (Mt. 18:11-14; Gal. 6:1). Sin cannot be tolerated in the church. The church must be concerned about maintaining sound doctrine. Those who would undermine the teachings of the church in any area (i.e. repentance, salvation, water baptism, work of Spirit, healing, etc.) should be dealt with. We are not to fellowship with "believers" who are in opposition to the truths of God's word, (II John 10-11; Rom. 16:17). We are to esteem Eldership highly, not receiving an accusation against them except with more than one witness, (I Tim. 5:19-20). Our attitude towards false doctrine should be to withdraw ourselves from people who live a disorderly life (that is, who are disordered due to being disobedient to the word of God) (II Thess. 3:6). We are not to argue or debate with legitimate leaders, (I Tim. 6:3-5).

We must not only refuse to listen to gossip, but let it be known that we are willing to take further steps to see that it is stopped, (Titus 1:10-11,13). Rather than encouraging gossip or accusation, we are to confront the rebellious, (II Thess. 3:14-15). Our attitude toward a weak brother should not be to judge but to receive and teach them the truth, (Rom. 14:1-4; 15:1). Christians should be counseled to only enter into covenantal relationships with believers, not only in marriage but in business as well.

God is a God of order and discipline. He orders and maintains discipline in heaven. He gave two clear Biblical examples of order and discipline. In the Old Testament, the children of Israel left Egypt and God immediately gave them order and discipline. In the New Testament, the early church received specific instructions on how to set up, organize and maintain bodies of people.

The disciplining of sinning members of the church is necessary for the spiritual health and strength of the body. A member of the church who falls into sin or who teaches false doctrine should be dealt with according to the principle and procedure given in Mt. 18:15-17; I Cor. 5:1-6, 11, 13.

Remember there must be witnesses. Before bringing the matter before the church, two attempts should have been made privately to bring about the repentance of the sinning member. In the bringing of a case for discipline before the church, the leadership is to take the initiative. If the difficulty is between two church members, the one who is in the right must initiate the restoration of fellowship. If bringing the case before the church does not lead to repentance, fellowship must be broken and he is to be regarded as a heathen. The leadership, under the direction of the Holy Spirit and prayer will determine any action to be taken, and it is then the responsibility of the congregation to support this judgment. When fellowship is restored between a repentant sinner and Christ and those whom he has offended, then the church cannot refuse fellowship. Before moving on, let me add on point of caution…none of what is mentioned above, other than to lovingly confront in a spirit of meekness, is to be applied to the new convert, or even to those who are honest strugglers with issues of sin in their lives. If a person is working with leadership to overcome, much grace, patience and love is needed on behalf of all…for many of us have been in similar places at different times, and the grace and love, rather than harshness and judgment won the day.

Blessed are the Peacemakers

We all have a responsibility in the Body of Christ to be peacemakers. Many problems can arise in church life. The Bible says, "Blessed are the peacemakers for they shall be called the children of God," (Mt. 5:9). The peacemakers' position is one of neutrality. It doesn't take sides. She/He is careful in giving advice. He/She helps to minimize problems, working to bring unity and strengthen families. Being trustworthy, confidential and caring is essential to fulfill the role of peacemaker.

Outreach

The whole Body has a responsibility to support the outreach ministries of the church. Every member of the Body has a place and duty to fulfill. However, we must never feel that we are the main hub around which the rest of the body must revolve, (I Cor. 12:18-27). We must be careful to give support to every area of ministry either in time, prayer or giving. We must continually pray for our missionaries. Missionary giving should receive equal importance with our generous offerings.

We also have a responsibility to those outside of the church. Our first responsibility to others is to bring to them the good news of the Gospel of Jesus Christ; the Gospel of the kingdom, (Acts 4:33; Rom. 10:14-15). We are an epistle, known and read of all men, (II Cor. 3:2). We, in loving friendship, are the primary way people will be introduced to Christ.

There are several ways we can deliver this message. First, by word of mouth, witnessing in testimony of what God has done for us. Second, by demonstration; through acts of kindness and love, as demonstrated in ethical conduct. In this generation, a truly honest person, one who has a high moral standard, stands out. By doing good to all men, without showing partiality in race or color or favoritism to one status group or another, but treating all men equally, we demonstrate Christ's love.

We are the light of the world! (Mt. 5:14, 16). We must be an example of righteousness in every action and word, (I Tim. 4:12). This includes having a pattern of good works, (Titus 2:7-8). We should not copy the behavior or customs of the world, (Rom. 12:2).

In fact, we are to live peaceably with all men, (Rom. 12:18). We are not to avenge ourselves or take the law into our own hands, (Rom. 12:19). We are not to take our brother to court or to ask an unbeliever to settle our differences, (I Cor. 6:1-4). We should make sure our speech is pure, (Col. 4:6; Eph. 4:29). We should always be kind and not angry or quarrelsome, (Eph. 4:31-32). We should not be greedy for this world's goods, (Heb. 13:5). We should not be contentious or argumentative, but give a simple yes, or no, (James 5:12). We should cheerfully share our home with those in need, (I Pet. 4:9). We should show a good attitude when we're mistreated or even abused, (I Pet. 4:14). We should be willing to lend what we have, even if there is no hope of return, (Luke 6:34-35). We must be an example to the world in all we say and do. I Tim. 2:9-10.

In our home, especially if there are unsaved members, our behavior should be Christ like. Jesus condemned the scribes and Pharisees for not honoring their father and mother by giving to them what was due but saying, "Corban", "I give what is due you, to God," (Mk. 7:9-13). We should never be guilty of using our service to the Lord as an excuse for neglecting our home and family. We must carry our share of the load in responsibility and in work. A happy home is our responsibility.

Our attitude in the home is also important. One of the greatest areas and training grounds for a Godly attitude is the home. We should demonstrate Christ's love, joy, patience, gratitude and appreciation, cheerfulness, contentment, honesty, diligence, kindness, obedience, sacrifice, service, forgiveness, loyalty and unity. Of course, no one is perfect, but this should be a goal to strive for.

The prophecy in Mal. 5:5-6 speaks of this day. The Lord desires to establish Christian homes that will be an example to the world and demonstrate his love and relationship between himself and his church.[9]

Duties as Parent's

There are a number of key duties of parents. They include: being an example, (I Kings 9:4; II Chron. 17:3); training and teaching, (Deut. 6:7; 4:9; 31:13; Prov. 4:3-4; Ex. 12:14; 26-27; Prov. 1:8, Prov. 22:6); providing for our children with, (II Cor. 12:14), nurture (Eph. 6:4), control (I Tim. 3:4), love (Titus 2:4), and correction (Prov. 13:24; 19:18; 22:15; 23:13).[10]

A mother's duties are myriad, and a Father's are of equal importance, but often, sadly neglected. Fathers are to rule with grace (I Tim. 3:12; 3:4), to discipline in love (Prov. 19:18; Prov. 3:12; Heb. 12:56), to correct (Prov. 22:15; 23:13), to teach (Deut. 6:7; 11:18-21; 4:9,10; Prov. 4:1-4; 1:8), to nurture; without provoking a child to anger (Eph. 6:4; Col. 3:21), to provide for our children (I Tim. 5:8; II Cor. 12:14), to encourage them in goodness (I Thess. 2:11), to tell them truth (Ex. 10:2), to guide them in their future vocation and righteousness (Jeremiah 3:4).

Similarly a Mother's Duty includes to correct (Prov. 29:15), with compassion (Is. 49:15), to comfort (Is. 66:13), with love (Titus 2:4), to teach (Prov. 1:8), with a gentle spirit (I Thess. 2:7).

Duties to Society

Every Christian is a member of society in the sense that he is

---

[9] For more on marriage, family and parenting, see Marriage and Family Life and Parenting on Purpose, by Dr. DeKoven.
[10] Ibid

part of the community in which he lives. The Lord has set us in our particular area to be a light even as he was, (John 17:18). We have a duty to our neighbors and our community to abide by the laws, to minister to their welfare, to help in trouble, and to be a blessing to them in any way we can. Jesus is our example. He went about doing good to every man. He only crossed the laws of his society when the laws of society were contrary to the Word of God, and to demonstrate the hypocrisy of the leaders in the community, (Luke 6:1-10).

As believers, we are to be faithful to our governments, by paying our fair share of taxes, (Rom. 13:6-7) and praying for, obeying and honoring government leaders and officials, (Rom. 13:1, Rom. 13:5; Titus 3:1; I Pet. 2:13-17). Again, Jesus is our example. He paid his taxes, (Mt. 17:27), and gave honor to the government, (Mark 12:16-17).

As a citizen of a nation, service in the military may be required as a civic duty. Depending on the nation raised in, mandatory service may be required, or voluntary. Many can serve in other capacities in the military, i.e. office work, medical duty, etc... There is always the possibility of filing as a conscientious objector if by personal conviction the individual cannot serve in the armed services. Every young person who faces this decision must come to their own conviction before the Lord. This is no easy decision, but objecting to war due to conscious does not mean that the person doing so is any less a citizen and patriot than one who willingly, and with zeal goes to war. The church should stand behind any decision well thought through and based upon a clear and settled conscience.

To Vote

We are blessed with the opportunity to vote for our leaders. Therefore, it is our duty as good citizens and our responsibility as Christians to acquaint ourselves with the various candidates and issues and, with much prayer for guidance, vote our convictions.

Of course, one must be careful not to be so focused on political issues and causes that one ignores other duties and responsibilities. Aligning oneself with a certain political party can also be unwise, as all political parties are a part of the "world system"; none is perfect or will perfectly represent the views and values of Christians!

Loyalty to our country should be part of our lives and we should obey, with a heart of gratitude and respect all that our government requires of us, as long as it does not conflict with the principles of God's Word.

Employee Employer Relations

As employers we are to be considerate, reasonable and just, (Eph. 6:9; Col. 4:1). We should not show favoritism in our employment standards, (Philemon 16). Employees are to diligently serve those who are over them, (Eph. 6:5). They are to do so with a healthy attitude, recognizing that they are doing it as unto the Lord. John the Baptist gave strict instruction to the servants of that day in Luke 3:14. They were to avoid mistreating workers, deal with them truthfully, while being content with their wages, while trusting God to provide and promote in His timing.

In humility as believers, we are to suffer patiently when wrongfully accused or abused, (I Pet. 2:18-20). Four attributes should be found in every Christian employee or employer, they are: humility, which is freedom from pride and arrogance (Prov. 8:13), meekness or patience under pressure is essential (Mt. 11:29; 5:5), our hearts should be respectful, as inward respect brings outward results (Eph. 4:15), and finally, we should act with courtesy, the outward result of respect (Col. 4:6).

Faithful Friends

We also have obligations to our friends. The Lord will hold us responsible, especially for those under our influence. The scripture reveals that a friend loves at all times and a brother is born for trouble, (Prov. 17:17). "A man that has friends must show himself friendly..." (Prov. 18:24). Our friends need us most in times of trouble. What an opportunity to show the grace and love of Christ, (John 15:13). Being a good friend means that we want the best for one another, thus a friend does not condone sinful patterns that are not repented for. A true friend speaks the truth in love and encourages their friend to live well, in accordance to biblical principles, (Prov. 27:6).

Enemy Enmity

Love is uniquely expressed in how we behave towards those in opposition to us. We are to pray for our enemies and earnestly seek their welfare, (Mt. 5:44-46). We should never harbor grudges or seek to harm or hope for calamity. We are to feed them, give them drink, bless them and pray for God to prosper them, (Rom. 12:14, 20-21). Of course, this is easier said than done.

Social Responsibilities

We need to be careful that we fulfill all of our social responsibilities, that we don't offend, (Eccl. 3:1, 4; Rom. 12:15). We need to learn to rejoice with those that are rejoicing and weep with those that weep, (Rom. 12:15). It is our responsibility to attend weddings, funerals, showers, birthday parties, etc. if at all possible; these are venues where our testimony for Christ can excel. We are responsible to each other as members of the Body of Christ, (Rom. 14:7; II Cor. 5:15).

Whatever responsibility we are given to do, the job should be completed as God gives strength. If we are in charge of a social function it should be planned out well, from greetings to clean up.

Our Christian Duty to Ourselves

Man is made up of body, soul and spirit. Each area must be

sanctified (set apart) unto the Lord, (I Thess. 5:23). "Do you not know that your body is the temple of the Holy Spirit?" We must take care of our physical temples. We are the only house that the Holy Spirit has to dwell in, and he can only minister effectively through them when they are in good health, (Rom. 12:1).

Part of good health is eating correctly. "You are what you eat". Make sure you have well-balanced meals so that you won't be short on proper nutrition. At the very least, supplementation of our diet with vitamins and minerals, and insuring that we monitor our health with regular check ups where possible is wisdom.

Everything about us must be clean, spiritually and naturally, (I Cor. 6:20). The natural is the only thing that men of the world see. Our outward appearance should testify of the inward cleansing in our lives. Even our houses, cars, job area, etc..., should be clean and neat as a testimony to the world. Our personal hygiene should be appropriate to the occasion.

Modesty in dress and demeanor are to be seen in all believers. Of course, standards of decency are different in different cultures, but we should err on the side of modesty.

We should not cause our brother or sister to stumble by exposing ourselves or dressing improperly in any way, (Rom. 14:21). "Blessed is he that watches and keeps his garments lest he be naked and they see his shame," (Rev. 16:15). We need to use wisdom in our personal style, and thought there is wide variation in our modern culture, any disciple of Christ will ask the question if their life style and choices are pleasing to the Lord.

It is also the Christian's duty to regulate and control the appetites of the body, (I Cor. 6:12). There are unnatural appetites, also the misuse of natural appetites, and excessive indulgence of natural appetites. It is God's order to keep every function of our bodies under control, (I Cor. 10:31).

Our souls, (mind, will and emotions) must be transformed and conformed to the likeness of Christ, (Rom. 12:1; Rom. 8:29). Our mind must be trained in:

- Knowledge. Knowledge of His Word, which is His will, needs to be studied, so that our beliefs begin to align themselves with God's, which will affect our emotions and behavior.
- Memory. To forget the things that should be forgotten and remember the things that should be remembered. Our healthy memories should be expanded daily by storing up portions of God's Word.
- Reflection. To meditate on the Word, day and night and to digest the teachings that we hear will begin to change us from the inside out.
- Emotions. To develop right feelings and to keep from reacting according to past feelings or experiences, but according to our new nature.
- Will. To make the right choices according to the Word of God and not according to past habits or wrong beliefs.

Our minds must be renewed in spirit (breath, rational soul, vital principles, and disposition). We need to let the breath of the Holy Spirit blow (blast) away our old thinking patterns. We need to think positively (Phil. 4:8), with a disciplined mind (I Pet. 1:13). We need to expel from our minds every thought that would lift itself above the truth of God's word or dilute our good conscience.

Our behavior patterns will change as our minds are transformed. We will no longer walk or behave ourselves according to the vanity (emptiness) of our own minds, but will have the mind of Christ, (Eph. 4:17-25). Thus, the Lord does not want us to use our inherited weaknesses as an excuse for not doing His will, (Titus 1:12-13). Bad habits can no longer co-exist with the perfect spirit of Christ, as we discipline our mind, say no to ungodly passions; we will please the Lord and live a good example for all.

Any weaknesses in bodily control or mental discipline will be corrected as our spirits are yielded to the spirit of Christ, (Rom. 6:13). Spiritually, we are to clothe ourselves with the garments that Christ has provided to make us strong and mature into his image, (Eph. 6; Ps. 18:34-37). This is taught by metaphor by Paul, as he presents the importance of wearing our armor. This includes:

- Loins girded with truth - strength through embracing and living the truth; while putting on…
- The breastplate of righteousness, which means a pure, clean heart;
- Feet covered with the preparation of the gospel of peace, indicating a disciplined walk;
- The shield of faith; believing, trusting, a positive confession;
- The helmet of salvation, a redeemed mind; and the
- Sword of the Spirit, becoming skilled in the teaching of God's word.

We are to put off anger, wrath, malice, blasphemy, filthy communication, the old man with his deeds (Col. 3:8-9), and put on the new man, filled with mercy, kindness, humbleness of mind, meekness, longsuffering, forbearance, forgiveness, love, peace, and thankfulness (vs. 10-15).

The Lord desires balanced characteristics in our spirit and personality, (Rom. 12:9-21). What needs to be developed in us are strong characteristics such as the hating of evil; generosity toward others, etc. There are gentle characteristics such as love, kindness, hope, patience, humility, which must be put on and practiced daily. There should also be a balance between doctrine and practice i.e., justice and grace, firmness and kindness, faith and works, worship and service, hearing and doing.

Above all we must accept ourselves as the Lord made us - with all our weaknesses and inadequacies - as well as our strength and abilities and be thankful.

Forms of Pleasure

A certain amount of pleasure in its proper place is undeniably right and proper and has the approval of God. The Lord went to a wedding feast (John 2:1-10), mixed with people on a friendly basis (Mt. 11:19), and attended dinner parties (Luke 5:29; 10:38-40). Paul speaks with evident approval of attendance at dinner parties in (I Cor. 10:27), even when believers are the guests of unbelievers.

We must not condemn all pleasure as ungodly. On the other hand, we must be cautious and exercise thoughtful and prayerful discrimination.

Specific Issues

Some ethical problems which we face today are specifically and directly treated in the Scriptures. Other present day problems, such as smoking, are not treated specifically and directly. In these cases, the question should be solved by the application of principles which are stated in Scripture.

The question of drinking is of great concern to many. The problem or question of ethics here really lies in the area of "social drinking". All Christians would agree that drinking to excess is wrong in the light of Scriptures, (Prov. 20:1; 23:29-35; I Cor. 5:11). There are many who maintain that the Bible condones drinking in moderation.

Remember, everyone is different, and some are more susceptible to the effects of alcohol than others. So, what should be the attitude of a believer? Paul's attitude and instruction seems more than adequate. In Romans 14: 14-17 Paul provides perspective. He chose to be conscious of the weak brothers, avoiding anything that might make them lose faith in Christ. At the same time, he had liberty to enjoy all the Lord had created, his conscience was clear. Public conscience is a matter to consider, and where drinking is considered by unbelievers to be inconsistent with a Christian's testimony, we should be especially careful.

There are many other forms of entertainment, from dancing to TV to movies to internet to music, etc. None of the above mentioned activities are evil in themselves, but one must be careful. The fact is, compromise with the world is so easy. Therefore, a believer needs to do all they can to avoid besetting sins and weights (Heb. 12: 1, 2), addictions and entertainment that causes ones mind or behavior to become less Christ like.

Open displays of affection amongst unmarried couples is common in our culture. This is a past time that it is altogether too common among young Christian people. Engaged couples must exercise extreme caution to keep familiarities within a minimum. Intimacies between young people who are not engaged is not a harmless pastime, but those who engage in them are playing with sexual fire. In many instances, it eventually leads to sin. Even though it may not lead to an overt act of sin, much damage can be done to both persons involved. Psychological and spiritual problems can come from unrequited love, immature acting out and giving in to sinful practices. The focus of a relationship dramatically shifts once the barrier of intimacy is violated.

A Final Thought

Paul stated in Phil. 4:8-9 to think on "whatsoever things are pure, whatsoever things are lovely, whatsoever things are of good report". What we think on is what will eventually dominate our lives. To fear the Lord, that is, consider what He wants rather than what we want, and being concerned about offending our Lord, will keep us on track. With this in mind, we move to the final four chapters, which present some biblical answers to the burning question; What does God want?

Chapter 6

What Does God Want- Ask of Me

By way of reminder, this work was begun as a question. The question came from listening into the prayers of the saints (and myself way too often), finding that most prayers were concerned about me, myself and I. I began a biblical search for the priorities of God; essentially, what does God want? In response to this most important question, I first visited the famous conversation between God the Father and the pre-incarnate Christ in Ps. 2: It reads

"Ask of Me, and I shall give the nations *for* Your inheritance; and the uttermost parts of the earth for Your possession." (Ps. 2:8, NKJV) Another version states, "What do you want? Name it: Nations as a present? Continents as a prize?" The Message Bible.

Listening in To Those with Influence

I remember as a child being invited in, on rare occasions, to the adult world. Mom (but usually Dad) would have a friend or friends over to the house, and I would sit and listen to the conversation. The dialog was often above my comprehension, but the thrill I felt just being included was overwhelming. Of the voices heard, the one I wanted to hear the most was that of my father. His strong, masculine voice was attended to above the rest; just because he was my dad.

As joyous as it was to listen in to my parents' conversation, how much greater would it be to listen in to the conversation between the Father and Son, as they discussed the future plans for all mankind. Well, in this passage of scripture we indeed have the privilege of listening in to this special conversation between the Father and Son. The discussion surrounded the purpose of the King and his Kingdom. In the heart of the King, and in the Son was to see the nations pay homage to the King. It was a conversation filled with emotion, with mutual respect and admiration.

The Father declares that the faithful Son can ask for whatever he wants. The Son, desiring to please the Father asks for the nations. This is his prayer, and should be ours as well. Of course, the answer is assured; in His time.

Prayers like this lead to an expression of true identity. The fact is, the Father was proud of the Son, and the Son wanted to honor the Father. Like Father, like Son, like his sons and daughters. The nations need Christ. There is a heaven to gain, and a hell to shun as the old phrase goes, and the responsibility of the church is to give all people groups the opportunity to have life in Christ. It is truly unethical to withhold the path to life from the nations. For in Christ we find the hope of the present and future.

What do you mean Ask?

The word to ask in this passage is the word Sha'al, a word with multiple meanings, including inquire, request, demand, beg, borrow, lay to charge, consult, desire earnestly, obtain leave, lend, pray. In this passage there are four emphases of this word. Each gives a picture of the purpose of God for our asking.

Fearsome Foursome

- Like a daughter with her daddy.

I have two delightful daughters, both grown with children of their own. When they were small, they learned at an early age how to get from their dad whatever they wanted (within reason). They smiled, asked "daddy" for something, and hoped for a positive response. My heart, easy as it was, wanted to give what they wanted, as long as it was in their best interest. They asked knowing my heart was already inclined towards them. It was my joy to give.

- A demand for something we have a right too.

David cried out in Ps. 4: 1, "Answer me when I call, O God of My righteousness (right). There are times when we must go beyond just asking for "a sure thing", and ask with passion and conviction. David recognized that there were promises the Lord had made to him, and he had a right to see the relief and grace of God. In similar fashion, we need to ask of the Lord for the promises he has made to us. The promises include the nations of the world; salvation for our loved ones, help for our neighbors, provision for our daily lives. Asking for what God has promised will indeed bring about the results of answered prayer; in the Lord's time.

- Asking for wisdom and strategy.

Not everything important to the Lord happens over night. In fact, the Lord is patient, and has waited for generations to see His Kingdom come in fullness. Often we need to ask, especially when a solution is not readily at hand for the specific strategy, and the wisdom to know how to bring about an answer from the Lord. In every nation, the strategy for winning the lost and discipling them to maturity is going to be different. Our prayer must be to hear the voice of God, and develop necessary strategy, as the task the Lord has given us is vital.

- Weep and cry for something due to the injustice and the need.

In Luke 18: 1-8, Jesus tells the story of an unrighteous Judge and a widow with a just cause. The picture presented is about persistence. There are some things that are worth praying for and praying for and praying for (and acting on) until the only acceptable answer comes.

I am reminded of the great crusader William Wilberforce (24 August 1759 – 29 July 1833), the British politician, philanthropist, and abolitionist who led the parliamentary campaign against the slave trade. He relentlessly fought for the abolition of slavery, seeing it finally abolished after 20 years of fighting. It was a just cause, worth giving all he had too. There are some things that require significant feet to our prayers. Issues for some like abortion on demand, infanticide in general, female genital mutilation, poverty, continued racism, etc. are worth fighting for or against, according to the convictions of heart. These ethical issues, and many others, are worth praying and fighting for until "justice roll down like waters And righteousness like an ever flowing stream." (Amos 5:24)

Chapter 7

What Does God Want- The Moses Mandate

A natural follow up to our question prompting our study is, what does God want from me? In this chapter we will explore what I have titled *The Five Point Star.* In De 10:12 we read; "An now, Israel, what does the Lord your God ask of you, but to *fear* the Lord your God, to *walk* in all His ways, and to *love* Him, and to s*erve* the Lord your God with *all* your heart and all your soul."

This five point star of a successful walk starts with…

The Fear of the Lord

The fear of the Lord speaks about reverential respect of the Lord, for certainly He is worthy of our honor and respect, demonstrated in a number of ways, to include living a life of…

- Wisdom (Job 28:28, Pr 9:10)-

The bible states that the fear of the Lord is the beginning of wisdom (not the end of it, for wisdom grows as our relationship with the Lord grows). Wisdom is defined as the ability to know what is right, understanding the principles of the word of God and applying truth to a given situation. Wisdom is definitely needed in life, and if we are to do what God wants, we will require wisdom from above, which is freely available to those who ask. (James 1:5). As alluded to above, we also need…

- Knowledge (Pr. 1:7)-

It takes knowledge of God to walk in wisdom and live according to the ways of the Lord. What is most needed in terms of knowledge is the principles of God's word, as found in a clear reading and understanding of scripture. Along with knowledge, we also need a life of…

- Worship (2 Ki. 17:36, Ps 89:7, 114:7)-

God is creator, sustainer, Father, Savior, King of our lives, and worthy of praise and adoration. More than singing, our life of service should reflect our worship of the Lord. Awe (Ps 33:8) is a part of worship, where we recognize truly how awesome God is in His attributes, His glory, His splendor and wonderful grace. Living in awe of God, as we worship Him leads us to the recognition of our…

- Duty to serve Him while serving others and leads to…

Blessings, such as:

- The ability to avoid sin (Ex 20:20)
- Long Life (De. 6:2, 24)
- Direction and peace (Ps. 25:12)
- An Inheritance (Ps 25:13)
- Covenant (Ps 25:14)
- Deliverance and preservation (Ps 33:19)
- Mercy (Ps 103:13)
- Fulfillment (Ps. 145: 19
- Health (Pr. 3:8)
- Confidence and Shelter (Pr. 14:26)
- Being remembered by God (Mal. 3:16)
- Receiving a Generational Blessing (Lu. 1:50)

Along with the fear of the Lord, we must learn to walk in His ways. Of course, to know His ways requires knowledge of the Word of God. It does indicate that there is a correct way to walk. Jesus said that he was the way, and is the way maker (the door). In following Christ and His teachings, we begin to fulfill Moses Mandate of walking in the ways of the Lord.

Part of walking in the way is to walk in love for God and others. More will be discussed on this in our last chapter. Suffice it to say for now that our ultimate goal, the goal of instruction is love, agape love, unselfish God like love for the Lord and His creation. (see 1 Tim. 1:5)

Love is demonstrated in service to others. Jesus set the standard extremely high when he used an outcast Samaritan as an example of love for others. Rubbing the lack of care for the wounded in the nose of the Pharisees was certainly one of Christ' goals, but primarily He desired that His disciples learned a different level of love…truly love of the same quality of His Father. Of course, love was to be with passion, with all ones being, not mere sentimentality, or just altruistic service, but passionate, and compassionate love for others was the requirement of the people of God, the mandate of Moses, but only realized by the Holy Spirit living through a believer.

Chapter 8

What Does God Want- It is the Walk

The Three Point Play

Mighty Micah the Old Testament prophet states; "He has shown you oh man what is good. And what the Lord does require of you but to do justice and to love mercy and to walk humbly with your God."

Provided here is the three point play of a successful walk, which starts with...

Justice

God is the God of the oppressed; he is the refuge for the poor (Ps. 14:6, Is. 25:4). As such he hears them (Ex. 22:27; Ps. 34:6), provides for them (Ps. 68:10; 82:3; 102:17; Is. 41:17), and secures justice for them (Ps. 140:12). All mankind has been and will be judged correctly and judiciously by the King, Christ (Is. 11:4). God has always had a special heart for the poor, providing such things as gleaning rights (Lev. 19:10), a cloak for security, which was to be returned at night for sleeping (Ex. 22:26-27, Deut. 24:12-13), daily payment of wages (Deut. 24:14-15), requiring an annual tithe be taken for the care of the poor (Deut. 14:29), along with many other provisions of scripture. Thus, the poor deserved impartial judgment and appropriate consideration, respect and care. (See "Christian Ethics in the Portable Seminary, 2006)

Justice is defined as... being just, the rendering of what is due or merited, and conformity to the law of God...an attribute of God. A second view is that by which we measure right and wrong; a verdict or sentence. The bible word comes from a root Hebrew word *Mish Paw*, meaning an open gate. Justice is a key biblical concept, strongly related to righteousness.

"Righteous and Justice are the foundation of God's throne,

loving kindness and truth go before You." (Ps. 89:14) Further, "Evil men do not understand Justice, but those who seek the Lord understand all things (Pr. 28:5). Finally, the prophet Amos states; "Let Justice roll down like rivers, and righteousness like an everflowing stream." (Amos 5:24) Righteousness and Justice are linked. For righteousness and justice to be seen in the church and beyond requires…

Mercy

Mercy is defined as kind and compassionate treatment of an offender, adversary or prisoner in ones power; to be kind, forgiving or helpful. It comes from a root Hebrew word *"Khe Sed"*, meaning beauty, mercy, kindness, a good deed and pity. In context, mercy assumes one has resources to meet a legitimate need, and takes the appropriate action to alleviate the problem or situation, often of injustice. If one does not have the means to help, he or she cannot be held accountable to act in mercy, for mercy is not a feeling, but an action from one able to help by God's grace from their resources. As with justice and righteousness, mercy and peace are linked, which will be discussed below. Mercy is seen in scripture…

- Like a father, demonstrating compassionate care for one of his own (Ps 103: 13). Biblically, since mercy is not natural to us, it…
- Must be practiced (Col. 3:12), with recognition that…
- You get what you give (Mt. 5:7), for…
- Judgment will be merciless to one who has shown no mercy; mercy triumphs over judgment." (Ja. 2:13), thus mercy should be a…
- Focus of Prayer, for our selves and others, the saved and the lost alike (He. 4:16).

Humility

Humility is defined as being free from pride of vanity; modest.

It is characterized by a person who is unpretentious, respectful. (Tsuna) This requires...

An honest self appraisal, which is realistic and accurate. God has created us with various gifts and abilities that we should rejoice in, as they are gifts from the Lord for the benefit of others. But scripture reminds us ...

- Before Honor comes humility (Pr. 15:33), for God resists the proud and gives grace to the humble (James 4:6)
- Peter states that we are to be clothed in humility, that is, we put it on as a part of our approach to the world (1Pe. 5:5,6), recognizing that
- Christ is our example (Phil 2: 5-13), and we are to follow Him.

Thus, we are to do justice, not just talk about it; love mercy, and demonstrate it with those in need, and live a life of humility, or as stated so eloquently by Paul the Apostle, we are to live as full members of Christ Kingdom now, characterized as **Righteousness Peace and Joy...all made available in the Holy Spirit!!**

What does God Want? Walk the walk, not just talk the talk, to live our lives as overcomers, with a heart of love.

Chapter 9

What Does God Want- It is all About Love

Life as an Overcomer

Jesus responds to a profound question "Teacher, which is the great commandment in the Law?" And He said to him, "You shall love the Lord your God with all your heart, and with all your soul, and with all your mind.' This is the great and foremost commandment. "And the second is like it, 'You shall love your neighbor as yourself.'

Love...God, neighbor, and self...What a concept! Love is talked about in many contexts, from a love of God, wife, country to sport and pizza. Perhaps the best teaching I have seen on this dynamic topic has been developed by my dear friend and ministry partner Dr. Ken Chant, who presents love from a Greek view, consisting of four words.

Eros...Wow, man!!

Erotic love is a blessing from the Lord when expressed in proper context. One cannot help but assume that when the Lord woke the man in the garden, and presented the woman in answer to his true need as acknowledged by God, did more than wax poetic, but exclaimed in incredible delight...Wow! Man! Thank you Jesus!. Romantic love, wonderful, precious, if not a bit unstable, is nonetheless a part of the love the Lord allows us to experience in this life. Of course, this is not what Jesus was talking about in context of this scripture.

Philea...Hey Brother, Where art thou!

Brother and sister love, fidelity and loyalty is important and wonderful. The love and protective care that is felt between brothers, whether in the natural expression or in the body of Christ is beautiful, but again, not what Jesus was alluding to in this passage.

Storge...We are family, all my brothers sisters and me

Family love was put in perspective by Jesus (see Matt. 12:46-50); important, but secondary to relationships in the Kingdom of God. Our loyalty to mom and dad, even husband and wife, important as they are, are secondary to our love for God and others... demonstrated in agape love.

Agape...Love you like the Rock of Ages

Agape is unselfish love, with a willingness to give to others before self. But scriptures do not state we are to passively express love, but we are to do so with...

Heart and Soul

From the center of our being to the center of another's, we are to express our love, as Christ did, as a demonstration of our sanctification. (1 Thess. 5:23) This type of love requires effort, and balance of all four loves presented above, requiring...

A Neighbor to Love

Jesus asked the question (paraphrased) who is our Neighbor? (Lu 10:30-37) It is often the undesirable, the unlovely that God challenges us to love. In Jesus teaching, the religious would have thought it impossible to fulfill this requirement, and with man, it is, but with God, all things are possible. Of course, in many ways...

Only Nuts Should Apply

That is, you have to be a bit radical to love the way Jesus did.

But we are no closer to having the mind of Christ than when we radically love the difficult amongst us.

Loving Me Loving You

To love like this requires humility, God working in us to will and do (Phil 2: 13) his good pleasure. Love of this type, unselfish agape love must flow from a person settled on who they are in relation to God and others. We must remember that all people are God's creation...including oneself! For we are all fearfully and wonderfully made, in God's image, for His pleasure, and we have the privilege of serving one another as an expression of God's love for all. (Ps. 139:14)

Jesus the Model

Jesus is our model, a man of actions vs. the religious words of His contemporaries, and he wants us to defy logic as well, and love with a passion, because he first loved us. (See Mark 3: 1-6)

What does God Want?

To see the completion of all that was lost in the fall restored to his creation. In fact, He completed the work on the cross. It is now the responsibility of the church to take our marching orders from him, and live a life of ethical purity, as overcomers in and through Christ, by the preaching of the Word of God and a demonstration of God's love in the word.

"And they overcame him, by the Blood of the Lamb, and by he Word of their Testimony, and they did not love their own life, even unto death." (Rev. 12:11)

We were born to overcome...we over come all things through love.

Concluding Thoughts

Recently, a Korean student, obviously driven by a mind out of control, killed 33 students in a senseless act of brutality. What should be done? Abortion remains a scourge in Western cultures, as millions of unborn are murdered each year. Wars rage, AIDS is wiping out areas of Africa, genocide remains the lot of many, and mental illness is seemingly growing around the world. What are we to do? How do we respond to the homeless, the hurting, the lost and disfranchised? Each person must make their own decisions, but should certainly consider the principles of the Word of God, many of which are discussed in this book. It is past time for the church to refocus our prayers, our concern, and our passion on being and doing what God wants...the highest calling is to glorify God, and we do this best when we live aligned with God, acknowledging and enjoying His presence, in full light of His wonderful word.

Vision International Educational Network

Vision International Education Network is a dynamic ministry for the local church, providing training and educational services to the body of Christ in the United States and in over 150 nations of the world. These services include:

- Academic and Vocational degree programs designed to prepare men and women for professional service in Christian Ministry and Community Service.
- Church based and On Line Learning programs to Equip God's people for effective services in the church and the marketplace.
- Vision publishing services, offering full service publishing for unique books designed to equip and train men and women for service. This includes the development and publishing of new books, along with the over 100 existing books available in multiple languages.
- The Vision Group provides consulting services to local churches, businesses and NGO's world wide with special emphasis on church growth and extension, church planting strategy, leadership development and team building, through their team of highly qualified and seasoned professionals on 5 continents.
- **Vision International Bible College in A Box** – complete educational programs offered through the World Wide Web and via CD. Transfer of credit allowed to Vision International Educational Network affiliated colleges and universities, for diploma/degree recognition. A two year program on side by side translated video or DVD is available in multiple languages through our affiliated International School of Ministry.

For more information contact:
Dr. Stan DeKoven, President
Vision International University
Vision International Education Network
Ramona, CA 92065
760-789-4700 or 1-800-9VISION
www.vision.edu
info@vision.edu
www.drstandekoven.com

www.ingramcontent.com/pod-product-compliance
Lightning Source LLC
LaVergne TN
LVHW051705080426
835511LV00017B/2738